# TYRANTS

## HISTORY'S 100 MOST EVIL DESPOTS AND DICTATORS

# TYRANTS

## HISTORY'S 100 MOST EVIL DESPOTS AND DICTATORS

### NIGEL CAWTHORNE

This edition published in 2024 by Arcturus Publishing Limited
26/27 Bickels Yard, 151–153 Bermondsey Street,
London SE1 3HA

AD011623UK

Printed in the UK

# ◄ CONTENTS ►

# ◄ INTRODUCTION ►

Most people cherish their liberty, though we are often rightly critical of the political and legal systems we have adopted to maintain it. Democracy is an imperfect tool. Indeed, as Winston Churchill said: 'Democracy is the worst form of government except for all those other forms that have been tried from time to time.'

One of those forms of government is tyranny. And Churchill had first-hand experience when it came to tyrants. He faced and defeated Adolf Hitler and Benito Mussolini, while allying himself to Josef Stalin during World War II, then opposing him in the Cold War.

Of course, this great triumvirate were not the first tyrants. Since the beginning of recorded time there have been men – and sometimes women – who have seized absolute power over a country. The first one covered here dates back to the 14th century BC. He thought he had the power to change the religion of an entire people, though he ultimately failed. Even so, he has not been alone in this ambition. Some tyrants even seek to make themselves gods and often believe that they have succeeded. Even Hitler identified himself with Christ. The comparison was not lost on his followers who saw him as the saviour.

To have such dizzying ambition invites opposition. To attain it means that all opposition must be ruthlessly suppressed. Consequently the tyrant must assume the power of life or death over their subjects. Those who oppose their will must die. And not just one person, but thousands, even millions. As Stalin said: 'A single death is a tragedy, a million deaths are a statistic.' Historians reckon that Stalin was responsible for the deaths of 20 million or more.

The great tyrants of the mid-20th century were not the end of the line. The world had not learnt its lesson. Tinpot dictators flourished in Latin America, often propped up by the United States which saw them as a bulwark against Communism.

Western democracies frequently dealt with very unpleasant dictators in former colonies for the same reason, or to continue exploiting the resources that first drew their interest in the colonial era. Where money is involved, human rights violations are often overlooked. We all have blood on our hands.

The question is: Are things getting any better? The answer is: Probably, but even so they are getting better rather too slowly.

So what can we do about it? Well, one thing we can do is to attempt to learn from history. We need to study the tyrants in the past and see whether we can detect the warning signs. Remember that most modern dictators – even Hitler – were voted into office.

Even such an enduring democracy as the United States is showing dangerous instability. In his 2004 novel *The Plot Against America* Philip Roth imagines Charles Lindbergh, the first man to fly the Atlantic solo and fan of Hitler, winning the 1940 presidential election, signing pacts with Nazi Germany and Imperial Japan, and beginning the persecution of the Jews. America is only saved from worse when Lindbergh's plane goes missing. These days, this sounds all too convincing.

Nigel Cawthorne
*Bloomsbury, October 2023*

# THE ANCIENT WORLD

A tyrant is someone who seizes power in a state without a legal right, but then in the ancient world the law was ill-defined. It could be just the word of the ruler. There was a democracy in Athens – interrupted by Alexander the Great and others – and a republic in Rome which came to an end when Octavian became emperor as Augustus. Some tyrants may have come to the power by legitimate succession, only to usurp other institutions, including religion, to bend everything to their will. They could even make themselves gods. There could, of course, be benevolent rulers, but power tends to corrupt and absolute power corrupts absolutely.

# Akhenaton

◄ 1353–1336 BC ►

## PHARAOH OF EGYPT

Born Amenhotep, he was the son of the Pharaoh Amenhotep III, who had expanded the eighteenth dynasty's hold on Asia and Africa. In the sixth year of his reign, Amenhotep abandoned the old religion and embraced the monotheistic worship of the god Aton, taking the name Akhenaton, which means 'the one who serves Aton'.

He then imposed the new religion on the Egyptian people, building huge temples to the new god at Karnak, on the site of temples dedicated to the old gods. He moved his capital two hundred miles down the Nile, from Thebes to a place now called Armana. A new city called Akhetaton – which means 'Place of Aton's Effective Power' – was built there. In the process, he centralized government and the economy, appropriating large tracts of land and levying crippling taxes. Meanwhile, he sent his agents out across the kingdom to destroy the monuments and shrines of the old gods.

However, the bureaucracy became corrupt, the army was neglected and he lost most of the territorial gains made by his father. When he died, he was succeeded by Tutankhaton, who, in a public repudiation of Aton, and a return to the old god Amon, whom Aton had temporarily replaced, was forced to change his name to Tutankhamon.

## Life and Crimes

**1353 BC**   Becomes Pharaoh of Egypt.

**1345 BC**   Takes the name Akhenaton and begins to force new monotheistic religion on Egypt.

**1336 BC**   On his death, Egypt repudiates the new religion and returns to old gods.

# Sennacherib

◄ Died 681 BC ►

## KING OF ASSYRIA

When Sennacherib succeeded his father Sargon II on the throne of Assyria in 704 BC, the provinces of Babylonia and Palestine rebelled. Over the following years, Sennacherib led a number of campaigns to retake them.

The Palestinian uprising had been backed by the Egyptians, but Sennacherib's planned punitive invasion of Egypt was halted when, according to Herodotus, a plague of mice ate the Assyrians' bowstrings and quivers.

When a Chaldean king took over Babylon in 691 BC and used the city's wealth to buy the support of the neighbouring Elamites, Sennacherib attacked, defeating a joint Chaldean–Elamite army at Halule. He suffered such heavy casualties in the process, however, that it took his army two years to recover.

Then in 689 BC, he returned to Babylon – then the centre of world culture – attacked the city and destroyed it. The destruction was so complete that it shocked the ancient world. Prisoners of war were used as forced labour to rebuild the city of Nineveh, Sennacherib's palace there and a city wall eight miles long.

Sennacherib was assassinated by his sons in January 681 BC. His memory is preserved as the subject of a poem by Lord Byron.

## Life and Crimes

704 BC   Succeeds his father as King of Assyria.

703 BC   Devastates the tribal areas of southern Babylon.

701 BC   Puts down uprising in Palestine.

691 BC   Defeats Chaldeans and Elamites at Halule.

689 BC   Razes Babylon.

681 BC   Assassinated by sons in January, probably in Nineveh.

# Pheidon of Argos

◀ died c.660 BC ▶

## TYRANT OF ATHENS

The word tyrant seems to have been brought into the Greek language just for Pheidon. The hereditary King of Argos in the eastern Peloponnese, he built up an army of massed infantry. In 669 BC, he defeated the Lacedaemonians at Hysiae, bringing him into conflict with the Spartans, who considered themselves the traditional slayer of tyrants. Pheidon defeated them and went on to take Athens.

At the same time the city of Aegina, which had built up its naval strength, was at war with Athens. Pheidon had allied himself with Aegina but, when Athens fell, he took Aegina too. It is said that he struck the first silver coinage there. He also introduced a standard system of weights and measures and many Greek cities, including Athens, adopted the so-called Pheidonian measures. In 668 BC, he intervened at Olympia and supported the Pisatans in their bid to take control of the Games from the Elians. He also tried to annex Corinth, bringing him into conflict with Sparta once more. Sicyon, Samos and Mitetus also seem to have fallen into his hands.

Aristotle described Pheidon as a tyrant because he depended for his power on military might rather than consent. In Argos power was concentrated in the hands of a single man, not spread among them. Pheidon seems to have been killed in the civil war in Corinth which produced that city-state's first tyrant. Other tyrants soon took power in Epidaurus, Megara and Sicyon.

## Life and Crimes

**669 BC**   Defeats Spartan army: declares himself sole ruler of Athens.

**c. 660 BC**   Killed in Corinthian civil war.

# Tarquin the Proud

## ◄ 564–505 BC ►

## LAST KING OF ROME

Lucius Tarquinius Superbus – 'Tarquin the Proud' – was the seventh and last king of Rome in ancient times. His father or grandfather Tarquinius Priscus had been murdered in 579 and succeeded by Servius Tullius. But Tarquin wanted the throne for himself. Murdering Tullius, his wife and brother in 534, he married the brother's wife and made himself king of Rome. He was an absolute despot and put many senators to death in the reign of terror that followed his accession.

Although he sought to curry favour in Rome with a series of wars against neighbouring Latin tribes, he was despised by the Romans, partly for his despotism, but also because he was an Etruscan. His costly building programme also alienated them. He removed the ancient Sabine shrines on the Capitoline Hill to make way for the Temple of Jupiter Optimus Maximus, a deity his family was associated with.

When Turnus Herdonius, the leading citizen of Aricia in Latium, tried to turn other Latin towns against him, Tarquin had him thrown into a pool of water with a wooden crate on his head. Stones were thrown into it until he slowly drowned.

Then, when the Latin city of Gabii resisted him, Tarquin sent his son there covered in bloody welts, claiming his father had mistreated him. This won the confidence of the citizens who put him in command of their troops. He then sent a messenger to his father asking how he should deliver the city into his hands.

The messenger found Tarquin walking in his garden. He made no reply to Sextus's query, but continued knocking the heads off the tallest poppies. To Sextus, the meaning was clear. He executed and banished the leading men of Gabii and the city submitted.

Then in 509, Sextus raped a noblewoman named Lucretia. She killed herself. The Romans rose up, led by the same Brutus family which would lead the assassination of Julius Caesar 500 years later, and expelled the entire Tarquinian clan. Tarquin fled to Etruria, and appealed for help in recovering his throne. An army led by Lars Porsena did succeed in defeating Rome, and annexing Roman territory, but stopped short of reinstating the monarchy and, for nearly the next 500 years, Rome was a republic, ruled by elected leaders.

# Life and Crimes

**564 BC**   Born son or grandson of murdered King Tarquinius Priscus.

**534 BC**   Murders King Tullius, his wife and brother; becomes seventh King of Rome.

**534–509 BC**   Absolute ruler of Rome: murders all those who oppose him.

**509 BC**   Son Sextus rapes Lucretia; family expelled from Rome.

**505 BC**   Dies in exile.

# Alexander the Great

### ◄ 356–323 BC ►

## KING OF MACEDONIA

Alexander the Great was such a bloodthirsty tyrant that he is portrayed in the Bible (Book of Daniel) as 'The Third Beast' who unleashes a bloody tide of slaughter on mankind, and in the Koran as 'The Two-Horned One' who will ravage the earth again with Satan in the last days.

He began his tyrannical career in 340 BC when his father, Philip II of Macedonia, made him regent. The 16-year-old promptly put down a rebellion of the Maedi people in Thrace, seizing their principal city and renaming it Alexandropolis, after himself. Two years later he led a crucial charge at the battle of Chaeronea, slaughtering the elite corps of Thebes, the Sacred Band.

In 336 BC he succeeded to the throne of Macedonia, even though he was implicated in his father's assassination – Philip had recently married again and had a son who would have replaced Alexander as rightful heir. The child and his baby sister were both killed by Alexander's mother who, it is said, pushed them face down onto a brazier. Philip's new wife was also killed.

Greece rebelled. Alexander responded by razing Thebes to the ground. He had 6,000 of its inhabitants summarily executed and sold a further 30,000 into slavery. This brutal act brought the rest of Greece to heel. He then declared war on Persia, ostensibly in retaliation for the Persians' invasion of Greece almost 150 years before. However, his tutor Aristotle had taught him that barbarian peoples – such as the Persians – were fit only to be Greek slaves.

Alexander defeated a Persian force dug in along the river Granicus, butchering some 4,000 Greek mercenaries and selling 2,000 survivors into slavery. He faced the Persian king Darius at the battle of Issus, where estimates of the Persian dead ranged between five and ten thousand. He also took Darius's wife, whom he impregnated, his favourite eunuch, and his harem of 365 of the most beautiful women in Asia – one for each night of the year.

He went on to take the coastal towns around the eastern Mediterranean, destroying any who opposed him. The city of Tyre was willing to surrender, but refused to let him lead a religious festival there. In response, he stormed the city butchering soldiers and civilians alike. Women and children were burnt to death when he set fire to the temples in which they had taken sanctuary. Once the city was taken, 2,000 men of military age were crucified on the beach, and 30,000 people were sold into slavery. Then at Gaza, the entire male population was killed to a man and the Persian governor was dragged around behind a chariot until he was dead.

Alexander went on to take Egypt unopposed. Returning through Palestine, he reduced the city of Samaria to rubble, executing its leaders and anyone who fled. After defeating Darius again at the battle of Gaugamela, he took Babylon, the richest city in the Middle East, where his men enjoyed a five-week orgy before moving on to the Persian capital Persepolis, which Alexander burnt down, probably while drunk.

He continued to pursue the fleeing Darius, showing no mercy to those who got in his way. And when Darius was murdered, Alexander pursued his killers. When Alexander caught up with the principal regicide, Bessus, he had him stripped and flogged. Then his nose and ears were cut off and Bessus was crucified. As Alexander continued to travel east, he stabbed one of his most trusted generals and closest friends, Cleitus, to death in a drunken rage.

Styling himself 'lord of the world' Alexander began to adopt Persian ways and Greeks who refused to prostrate themselves before him Persian-style faced execution on the flimsiest of charges. He uncovered various 'plots' and purged the army of anyone whose previous allegiance had been to his father. The conspirators were tortured and stoned to death, or simply murdered. He opened and read his men's mail. Anyone who showed the slightest discontent was put in a special disciplinary company that was used for dangerous missions or to garrison remote towns.

He marched on into India, destroying cities and butchering the inhabitants as he went. At Massaga, the capital of the Assacenes, Alexander offered the 7,000 Indian mercenaries defending the city safe conduct, then slaughtered them along with their wives and children when they refused to join his army and fight their fellow countrymen.

At the river Jhelum, he faced the Indian king, Porus. Indian deaths in this battle were estimated at anything between 12,000 and 23,000, including the king's two sons. Alexander's army marched to the Beas river, where his men refused to go any further. Although Alexander assured them they were nearing the great Eastern Ocean which marked the end of the world, they could see the North Indian Desert and the Himalayas spread out before them. Alexander's empire now extended further than that of any Persian emperor and he had outstripped the achievements of even the Greeks' mythological heroes.

Instead of returning the way they had come, Alexander took his men south, crucifying the governors of towns that opposed him and hanging the Brahmins who encouraged resistance. At Multan, Alexander was wounded and the entire population of the city was massacred.

Alexander then marched his army along the Makran Coast and across the Gedrosian Desert – losing half their number, including all the women and children camp followers. Alexander's sole reason for making this attempt was simply that all those who had tried it before had failed. Back in Persia, he purged the governors whom he had left behind to administer the empire, killing some by his own hand.

When his Macedonian troops objected to the favour he was showing his Persian subjects, he had the ringleaders summarily executed. In a mass wedding, eighty of his commanders were married off to Persian princesses: Alexander himself married three. Meanwhile he sent instructions back to the Greek city-states that he was to be declared a god.

In 323 BC, Alexander died in Babylon at the age of 32 after a ten-day drinking binge. There is good reason to believe that he was poisoned. With no clear successor, his empire quickly disintegrated. Alexander's wars had killed off a large part of Macedonia's male population and had left the country so weakened that it was never to rise again.

## Life and Crimes

356 BC  Born on 20 or 26 July in Pella, capital of Macedonia.

340 BC  Crushes the Maedi.

**338 BC**  Slaughters the Sacred Band of Thebes.

**336 BC**  Implicated in the murder of his father.

**335 BC**  Destroys Thebes.

**334 BC**  Invades Asia.

**333 BC**  Defeats Persian king Darius at battle of Issus.

**332 BC**  Butchers the male populations of Tyre and Gaza, selling any surviving women and children into slavery; takes Egypt.

**331 BC**  Destroys Samaria; defeats Darius at battle of Gaugamela; takes Babylon.

**330 BC**  Burns down Persepolis while drunk; murders a number of his father's followers.

**329 BC**  Has Darius's killer mutilated and crucified.

**328 BC**  Murders his friend Cleitus in a drunken rage.

**327 BC**  Demands followers prostrate themselves before him, murdering those who refuse; invades India massacring those who oppose him.

**326 BC**  Defeats Porus at battle of Hypasdes; his army rebels after it is clear that Alexander intends to march on, killing and conquering to the ends of the earth.

**325 BC**  Massacres population of Multan; marches his men across Gedrosian Desert, half of whom die en route.

**324 BC**  Purges governors of Persia; murders Macedonians who oppose him; marries his commanders to Persian women; declares himself a god.

**323 BC**  Dies in Babylon after ten-day drinking binge; probably poisoned.

# Emperor Ch'in Shih-huang-ti

◄ c. 259 BC–c. 210 BC ►

## EMPEROR OF CHINA

Born Cheng Hsiang, he became ruler of Ch'in in north-west China at the age of 13. His prime minister Lü Buwei served as regent but was exiled when Cheng came of age in 236 BC. He then embarked on a brutal campaign to take over all the other feudal states of China.

Naming himself 'Shih-huang-ti' – which means 'First Sovereign Emperor' – he consolidated power by forcing all the important families to live in his capital Hsien-yang where he could keep an eye on them. Anyone who disagreed with him was executed. To prevent the dissemination of dangerous ideas, in 213 BC, he ordered the burning of all books, except those on farming, medicine and prophecy.

Obsessed with the Taoist idea of immorality, he sent hundreds of magicians to search for the legendary Isles of the Blessed, where the inhabitants were said to live forever, while hundreds more were set to work concocting the elixir of life. When they failed, he had 460 of them executed.

When his mother's lover attempted a coup, the emperor had him torn apart by horses. His entire family were killed, his army slaughtered and his supporters beheaded. Shih's mother was stripped of her position of Queen Dowager and held under house arrest until her death many years later, while the two sons she had had with her ambitious lover were beaten to death. Lü Buwei who had introduced the couple to cover-up his own dalliance with the queen – and may have been Shih's real father – committed suicide rather than face execution.

Fearful of assassination, the emperor withdrew to a vast palace, one of many built by 700,000 men drafted in especially for the task. It is not known how many were pressed into service to build what was to become the precursor to the current Great Wall of China. Meanwhile other walls separating the former warring states were pulled down to impose central rule. A massive new system of roads and the Lingqu Canal, joining the Xiang River flowing into the Yangtze and the Li Jiang flowing into the Pearl River, were built.

The emperor was so seldom seen that the precise date of his death, around 210 BC, cannot be determined. He was buried in a giant mausoleum in a mountain, guarded by 6,000 terracotta warriors. Although he boasted that his family would rule China for 1,000 generations, the Ch'in dynasty was extinct only a few years after Shih's death. The China he united, however, is still in existence 22 centuries later.

## Life and Crimes

**c. 259 BC**  Born in Ch'in, north-west China.

**246 BC**  Becomes emperor.

**236 BC**  Exiles prime minister and embarks on brutal military campaign to unite China.

**213 BC**  Burns all books, except those on farming, medicine and prophecy.

**c. 210 BC**  Dies in Hsien-yang.

# Herod the Great

## ◄ 73–4 BC ►

## KING OF JUDAEA

Born in Palestine in 73 BC, Herod was the son of Antipater, who was named procurator of Judaea in 47 BC by Julius Caesar as a reward for supporting the winning side in the civil war. This gave the whole family Roman citizenship.

Antipater made his 16-year-old son governor of Galilee, where Herod launched an unpopular campaign against local bandits.

The murder of Julius Caesar in 44 BC plunged the Roman Empire back into civil war and left Antipater and Herod short of money. The taxes they imposed caused an insurrection in which Antipater was killed; Herod, with Roman help, put down the rebellion and killed his father's murderer.

Herod managed to convince Mark Antony that the eastern provinces had supported him against Cassius and Brutus and was rewarded by being appointed tetrarch of Galilee, while his brother Phasael became tetrarch of Jerusalem.

An anti-Roman insurrection forced Herod to flee in 40 BC, while Phasael committed suicide and Herod's father-in-law Hyrancus, the King of Judaea, was taken into captivity in Babylon by the Parthians. In Rome, Herod managed to secure the backing of the Senate and in 36 BC he rode back into Palestine at the head of a Roman army and besieged and captured Jerusalem. The enemy fled into the hills and found shelter in caves. Herod pursued them, slaughtering men, women and children.

Herod persuaded the Parthians to release Hyrancus, but refused to give him back his throne. Instead Herod took the crown, using the presence of the old monarch to buttress his rule. He began an extensive building programme and minted coins with his likeness on them.

Herod was almost undone through his support for Antony and Cleopatra in their struggle against Octavian, but he quickly changed sides when it became plain he was backing a loser. He sailed to Rhodes to meet Octavian, after executing Hyrancus so he could not take the throne in Herod's absence. In a brilliant speech, Herod boasted of his loyalty to Mark Antony, then pledged the same to the new ruler of Rome. His audacity paid off and Octavian confirmed him as King of Judaea, it being clear that Herod would be a useful ally if Octavian had to pursue Antony and Cleopatra into Egypt. When Octavian became the Emperor Augustus, he rewarded Herod by giving him jurisdiction over Jericho and Gaza.

Herod ruled unchallenged in Judaea for thirty-two years. He rebuilt Jerusalem after an earthquake in 31 BC, built new fortresses to hold his territory and built a new port called Caesarea in honour of Augustus. The taxes he needed to raise to do this made him extremely unpopular. The old royal houses who he had deposed opposed him and the Pharisees condemned him for repeated violations of Mosaic Law. He was seen as a puppet of Augustus, who had offended the Jews by ordering that the priest of the Temple make sacrifices twice a day for Rome and the Senate. The Jews also believed that Herod, a pagan, was violating their graves and stealing gold objects from the tomb of King David. To hold on to power

*Herod's soldiers massacre the innocents in this engraving by Gustav Dore.*

he employed mercenaries and a secret police. He also married ten times for political reasons.

As time went by, Herod became increasingly mentally unstable. He murdered his second wife Mariamme, her two sons and her entire family, fearing that they were plotting against him. He also killed his first-born son Antipater, leading Augustus to remark that it was preferable to be Herod's pig (hus) than his son (huios).

In 8 BC, the monastery at Qumran, the home of the Essene sect, was destroyed by a fire thought to have been started by Herod: he also had a group of Jews burnt alive for removing from the Temple a golden eagle, which they considered a graven image.

Towards the end of his reign, Jewish scholars announced that seventy-six generations had passed since the Creation. It was well known that the Messiah would be born in the seventy-seventh generation. According to St Matthew's Gospel, Herod ordered the slaughter of all male infants after hearing that a child born in Bethlehem was being honoured as the king of the Jews. However, this is the only source for the story.

After an unsuccessful attempt at suicide Herod died in Jericho in 4 BC. His kingdom was divided among his surviving sons.

## Life and Crimes

**73 BC**   Born in southern Palestine.

**47 BC**   Becomes Roman citizen.

**41 BC**   Appointed tetrarch of Galilee by Mark Antony.

**40 BC**   Flees to Rome where he is named king of Judaea.

**36 BC**   Returns to Palestine at the head of a Roman army.

**29 BC**   Murders wife Mariamme, her two sons and all her family.

**4 BC**   Massacre of the Innocents; Herod dies March or April in Jericho.

# Augustus
## ◄ 63 BC–AD 14 ►
## FIRST EMPEROR OF ROME

Augustus Caesar was the first emperor of Rome. He sought absolute power ruthlessly and, when he attained it, sought to expand his empire so he that ruled the whole of the known world.

Born Gaius Octavius, his father was a Roman senator, who died when his son was four. Octavian, as he was known, came to public attention at the age of 12 when he made the oration at the funeral of his grandmother Julia, the sister of Julius Caesar. When he was 17, he accompanied Caesar on the triumphal procession after his victory in Africa and, the following year, fought with him in Spain.

Octavian was in military school at Apollonia in present-day Albania when Caesar was murdered. With his schoolmate Agrippa he returned to Italy, where he learnt that Caesar had adopted him and made him his heir before he died. However, Caesar's chief lieutenant Mark Antony believed himself to be Caesar's heir and refused to hand over Caesar's possessions.

Octavian then mounted a campaign to take power. First he raised money to pay off Caesar's debts, then he ingratiated himself with the Roman public by putting on games. With the support of the Senate, he joined the campaign against Antony, who was defeated and forced to withdraw to Gaul. Octavian then turned his troops on the Senate and forced them to confer a vacant consulship on him. By now he was calling himself Gaius Julius Caesar, and was acknowledged as Julius Caesar's son.

Octavian then formed a triumvirate with Mark Antony and Lepidus, the new chief priest and one of Caesar's supporters. It had dictatorial powers for five years, and enemies – including 300 senators – were ruthlessly purged. Although Antony was seen as the leading triumvir, Octavian's prestige received a boost when Caesar was elevated to the status of a god.

Armies under Antony and Octavian crossed the Adriatic to take on Brutus and Cassius, Caesar's principal assassins. Antony defeated Cassius, while Octavian lost to Brutus. But the combined forces of Antony and

*Ruler of the world, Caesar Augustus.*

Octavian defeated Brutus three weeks later. The republican cause was lost and Brutus and Cassius committed suicide.

Antony returned to Gaul, but Octavian defeated his brother and wife in the Perusine War. Sextus Pompeius, son of Caesar's enemy Pompey the Great, then sided with Mark Antony, but Antony made a fresh agreement with Octavian carving up the Roman Empire between them and limiting Lepidus's territory to Africa. Pompeius fought on alone, but was defeated by Octavian's friend Agrippa.

To seal the deal between Antony and Octavian, Antony was to marry Octavian's sister Octavia – although he had already spent the winter with the Queen of Egypt, Cleopatra. Meanwhile Octavian stripped Lepidus of his remaining territory. He now held the whole of the west, and foreign victories and public works made him popular with the people of Rome.

When Antony divorced Octavia to marry Cleopatra, Octavian declared war on Egypt, defeating the combined force of Antony and Cleopatra in a naval battle off Actium on the west coast of Greece. Octavian then pursued the couple back to Egypt, where they committed suicide. He executed Cleopatra's son by Julius Caesar, Ptolemy XV Caesar, and used her treasure to pay off his soldiers. Octavian then annexed Egypt, making him master of the Greco-Roman world.

Back in Rome, he established a Praetorian Guard to maintain his absolute control. The Senate made him emperor in 27 BC and gave him the title 'Augustus'. In the east he took Armenia as a protectorate, while Agrippa subjugated Spain. Caesar Augustus now centralized the administration of the empire in his own hands and sent armies north to extend the empire into Switzerland, Austria and Germany.

In 12 BC, he became pontifex maximus, head of the state religion, and in 2 BC he was made 'Father of His Country'. In AD 6, he annexed Judaea. He died on 19 August AD 14, and was made a god on 17 September.

## Life and Crimes

**63 BC**  Born 23 September at Velitrae near Rome.

**51 BC**  Delivers funeral oration for Julia, Julius Caesar's sister.

**46 BC**  Accompanies Caesar on his triumphal procession after victory in Civil War.

**44 BC**  Octavian returns to Rome where he finds he is the assassinated Caesar's heir.

**43 BC**  Octavian, Mark Antony and Lepidus form triumvirate.

**42 BC**  Julius Caesar declared a god, making Octavian the son of a god; Brutus and Cassius defeated at Philippi.

**36 BC**  Removes Lepidus from power, taking the entire Western Empire.

31 BC   Defeats Antony and Cleopatra at battle of Actium.

30 BC   Annexes Egypt.

27 BC   Takes name Caesar Augustus.

20 BC   Takes control of Armenia.

16–15 BC   Sends army across Alps, extending frontier to the Danube.

12 BC   Becomes pontifex maximus.

9 BC   Frontier extended to the Elbe.

AD 6   Annexes Judaea.

AD 14   Dies on 19 August.

# Caligula

◄ AD 12–41 ►

## EMPEROR OF ROME

Born Gaius Julius Caesar Germanicus, Caligula was brought up in the military camps of his father Germanicus and got his nickname – which translates as 'Little Boot' – after the army footwear he wore as a youth. His father died in AD 19, and his mother and two older brothers were executed by the Emperor Tiberius in political purges, but Caligula managed to ingratiate himself with Tiberius.

Caligula married the daughter of a nobleman in the hope that it would improve his chances of succeeding Tiberius. After losing his first wife in childbirth, however, Caligula seduced the wife of Naevius Sutorius Macro, commander of the Praetorian guard, even promising to marry her if he became emperor, while at the same time, he wormed his way into Macro's favour. According to Suetonius, Caligula then poisoned Tiberius, intending to seize power. When the poison did not immediately kill Tiberius, Caligula suffocated him with a pillow or strangled him, according to which source one reads. A freeman who had seen what had happened and cried out a warning was later crucified, on Caligula's orders.

The population of Rome was not sorry to see the back of Tiberius, and Caligula was a popular figure; his father being remembered with affection and the slaughter of Caligula's family earning him popular sympathy. He was also the first direct descendant of Augustus to come to the throne, which did him no harm at all.

Although initially popular, seven months after his accession Caligula fell ill and the fever seems to have affected his brain. After he recovered, he instigated a series of treason trials of his own. The following year, he forced Gemellus and his father-in-law Gaius Silanus to commit suicide after accusing them of treason. Caligula began to fear the growing power of Naevius Sutorius Macro, the prefect of the Praetorian Guard who had helped him to power. After sending Macro out of Rome to Egypt, under the pretext of making him governor of the province, Caligula had him arrested and executed.

Later that year, Caligula's favourite sister Drusilla, with whom Caligula had had an incestuous relationship since childhood, died. A season of public mourning was announced by Caligula, during which it was made a capital offence to laugh, bathe or dine with members of your own family. He minted coins in Drusilla's honour and had her deified, although her divinity was later revoked.

After the mourning was over, he took time off from running the empire and spent lavishly on games, banquets and public displays. He built a pontoon bridge three miles long across the Bay of Naples and rode back and forth across for two days. He built vast galleys, villas and country houses regardless of expense. Guests at banquets would find gold moulded into the shape of food on plates in front of them. He would dissolve valuable pearls in vinegar and drink down the mixture. Within six months he had squandered the vast fortune Tiberius had left.

To raise money, he started a fresh round of treason trials (those condemned of treason in Imperial Rome forfeited their property to the state). Caligula would name the amount he sought to raise at the start of each day's proceedings: in one particular afternoon he condemned as many as forty men to raise the desired figure, complaining afterwards what a tiring day he had had. He revoked the Roman citizenship of many who had earned it and seized their estates. Others were forced to name him as their heir, then were sent poisoned sweetmeats. Caligula also personally sold off the public properties left over after the games.

Caligula had men executed for little or no reason. His brother Tiberius was put to death without warning. Senators were executed secretly and he would continue summoning them as if they were still alive. His uncle Claudius, it is said, was spared only because he was considered a laughing stock. Criminals were fed to his lions, on the grounds that they were cheaper than butcher's meat. After an oratory competition, he forced the losers to erase their wax tablets with their tongues, on pain of death.

Caligula would have sex with any man or woman that took his fancy: a refusal on the 'lover's' part would have been distinctly unwise. He would then publicly recount in detail the performance of his lover. These lovers included a woman named Caesonia, who he liked to display naked to his friends. When she had a child, he married her: although Caesonia was notoriously promiscuous, the vicious way the little girl would scratch at the eyes of the children who played with her convinced Caligula that the child was in fact his.

Caligula's behaviour became increasingly disruptive to the smooth running of the city. He would close the granaries so that the people would go hungry, or scatter free tickets to the circus among crowds, causing stampedes where many people died. He put on contests between mangy beasts and people who were crippled or infirm. When one contestant complained, he had his tongue cut out before being returned to the arena. People were condemned to death in the arena without the case against them even being heard. A famous writer was burnt alive in the middle of the arena for some imagined offence and the manager of the gladiators was chained up and beaten for days on end, his torment only ending when Caligula could no longer stand the smell of putrefying brains.

Parents were forced to watch the execution of their own children. One man was brought on a litter when he pleaded that he was too ill to attend. Another was invited to dinner after the execution and Caligula tried to cheer him up. Men of rank were branded, shut up in cages like wild animals or sawn in half. He ordered one senator to be torn to pieces and his lust for cruelty was not sated until he saw the man's limbs, bowels and other body parts dragged through the street and placed in a heap before him.

He often ordered torture or decapitation as entertainment while he was eating. At the dedication of one bridge, he pushed a number of people into the water, using a boathook to make sure they drowned. He killed people with a cudgel simply for disturbing him at the games and beat sacrificial victims to death in the temple with a hammer. A slave who was accused of stealing had his hands cut off and hung around his neck, then was displayed at a party with a placard around his neck explaining what he had done.

In AD 39, Caligula went to Germany, where he discovered a plot by the military commander Gaetulicus to kill him and replace him with Aemilius Lepidus, the widower of Drusilla and lover of Agrippina the Younger. The two men were executed and Agrippina and Livilla were exiled.

The following year, Caligula invaded and plundered Gaul, and planned to invade Britain, even having triremes carried overland from Rome to cross the Channel. But when he reached the English Channel, he contented himself with ordering his men to collect seashells from the beach, which he called the spoils of the conquered ocean. Meanwhile he rebuked the Senate, accusing them of indulging in revels, going to the theatre and living comfortably in their villas while he was risking his life in battle.

Before returning to Rome, he tried to slaughter his own legions, ordering them to assemble without their weapons. When they realized what was going on, he was forced to flee. Despite this, he entered Rome in triumph. To pay for the parade he imposed new taxes on food, lawsuits, the wages of porters, marriage and the earnings of prostitutes – even those he had prostituted himself. He set up a brothel in his palace and forced people into prostitution, displaying them there naked. Patrons were lent money at extortionate rates. Details of his new taxes were not published. When he was forced to do so, the law appeared in tiny letters, posted up in a narrow corridor where it was impossible to copy. Later he took to straightforward confiscation, complaining that he was so poor that he could not afford a dowry for his baby daughter.

Caligula had pretensions to divinity and built temples and statues to himself. Statues of other noted Romans were destroyed and even those of Augustus moved. He even thought of destroying the poems of Homer, and he had Virgil's work banned from libraries. The certificates of deification of Julius Caesar and Augustus were old and out of date, he said. And he ordered his own statue to be placed in the Temple in Jerusalem so that the Jews could worship him, though the procurator of Judea procrastinated and the statue was not in place by the time of his death.

Caesonia plied Caligula with drugs to improve their lovemaking, which made him even more mentally unstable. He often wore women's clothing or dressed as a god with a blonde beard or as Venus or a triumphant general, wearing the breastplate of Alexander the Great which he had taken from his sarcophagus. He also caused a scandal, singing and dancing in public and appearing on stage with lowly actors.

Caligula was already in danger from the legions in Germany who had turned against him. Now he deliberately alienated those closest to him, threatening to kill them and himself if they thought he deserved death. Omens told of his forthcoming death and a performance of a play was staged, showing the murder of a king – in this case, Philip of Macedonia, Alexander the Great's father.

On 24 January AD 41, Caligula attended the Palatine Games, where he was stabbed at least thirty times by the tribune of the Praetorian guard and other high-ranking conspirators. As he lay writhing on the ground he was despatched, it is said, with a sword thrust through his private parts. His wife Caesonia was stabbed to death by a centurion, while his daughter's brains were dashed out against a wall.

Caligula was just twenty-nine and had ruled for less than four years when he was assassinated. His body was taken secretly to the garden of the Lamian family, partially burnt in a hastily constructed funeral pyre then buried. When his sisters returned from exile, they had it dug up and cremated properly, and the ashes placed in the family tomb. His uncle Claudius, whom Caligula had spared as a laughing stock, succeeded him as emperor.

## Life and Crimes

AD 12   Born 31 August at Antium, modern-day Anzio, Italy.

AD 19   Father dies.

AD 33   Mother and brothers executed.

AD 37   Murders Tiberius and usurps the throne.

AD 38   Executes legitimate heir and those who helped him to power.

AD 39   Executes brother-in-law; builds pontoon bridge across Bay of Naples.

AD 40   Plunders Gaul.

AD 41   Assassinated 24 January in Rome by the Praetorian guard and other high-ranking conspirators.

# Agrippina

◄ AD 15–59 ►

## 'EMPRESS' OF ROME

Agrippina the Younger was the great-granddaughter of the Roman Emperor Augustus and sister of the Emperor Caligula. In AD 39, Caligula exiled her for conspiring against him, but he allowed her to return to Rome in AD 41. In AD 49, Agrippina saw her main chance, and seized it. Poisoning her second husband, Passienus Crispus, she married her uncle, the Emperor Claudius, by then an old and feeble man.

Normally, in Roman society a man marrying his niece would have been considered incestuous and immoral, but convention was flouted and Aggripina effectively took control. Her rival for the hands of Claudius, Lollia Paulina, was accused of sorcery. Without being given a hearing, her property was confiscated and she was sent into exile where she committed suicide, reportedly on the orders of Agrippina.

*Agrippina poses for the sculptor with her son, the future Emperor and tyrant Nero.*

Agrippina soon bullied Claudius into adopting her son Nero, and strengthened Nero's position further by marrying him to Claudius's daughter Octavia after her former betrothal to Agrippina's second cousin, the praetor Lucius Junius Silanus Torquatus, was broken off when Silanus was accused of incest with his sister Calvina. Excluded from public office, Silanus committed suicide and Calvina was sent into exile. Agrippina then ordered the murder of Silanus's elder brother to prevent him taking revenge.

As wife of Claudius, she became his trusted adviser. In AD 50 she was given the title AVGVSTA, meaning 'empress'. Statues of her were erected across the empire and her likeness appeared on coins. She had her own court, signed official documents and, in the Senate, her followers were awarded with public offices and governorships. Potential rivals were poisoned, particularly anyone loyal to Claudius's previous wife Messalina.

It is very likely that she also murdered Claudius, who died in AD 54 after eating poisoned mushrooms, along with his son and heir Britannicus. Nero became emperor, but Agrippina held on to power as regent. However, her son soon realized that he was not safe from his mother's lust for power and tried to kill her. He attempted to poison her three times. Then he sent her out into the Bay of Naples on a ship designed to sink, but she managed to swim ashore. Eventually Nero sent soldiers to her villa to beat her to death.

## Life and Crimes

- **AD 15** Born in Rome.
- **AD 39** Exiled for plotting against her brother Caligula.
- **AD 41** Returns to Rome.
- **AD 49** Murders her husband and marries the Emperor Claudius.
- **AD 50** Becomes AVGVSTA.
- **AD 54** Claudius dies – probably murdered by Agrippina – and she takes power as regent.
- **AD 59** Murdered by her son Nero.

# Nero

## ◄ AD 37–68 ►

## EMPEROR OF ROME

With the possible exception of Caligula, Nero was the most unpleasant tyrant that the Roman Empire produced. Born Lucius Domitius Ahenobarbus, his mother Agrippina the Younger changed his name to Nero Claudius Caesar when she married her uncle, the Roman Emperor Claudius. When Claudius died in AD 54 – probably poisoned by Agrippina – the 17-year-old Nero was proclaimed emperor by the Senate and Praetorian Guard. Agrippina, however, effectively wielded power as regent.

By AD 59, Nero had grown tired of his mother and, after several failed attempts, murdered her. In AD 62, the prefect of the Praetorian Guard, Sextus Afranius Burrus, died and the Stoic philosopher Lucius Annaeus Seneca retired. They had been his closest advisers and a restraining influence.

Burrus was replaced with the infamous Gaius Ofonius Tigellinus, who had been exiled in AD 39 by Caligula for adultery with Agrippina, and Nero had already come under the influence of Poppaea Sabina, the former wife of two of his friends, who had become his mistress in AD 58. Poppaea encouraged Nero to murder his wife Octavia, the daughter of Claudius, and in AD 62, Nero married Poppaea.

At Tigellinus's instigation, a series of treason laws removed anyone considered to be a threat. Meanwhile, military setbacks spawned an economic recession, while Nero and his wife lived in extravagant style.

In AD 64 a fire left much of Rome in ruins. Although Nero himself commanded the fire fighting, it was said that he sang or played the lyre as he watched the city burn. There was also a rumour that he had started the fire himself to clear the way for an extravagant palace called the Golden House, built at a time when public reconstruction should have been a priority. The fire also became the excuse for the first persecution of the newly emergent Christians.

In AD 65 Nero appeared on stage and sang for audiences. This was the equivalent of a modern-day President of the United States appearing in

*Nero murdered his mother and during the great fire of Rome in AD 64, citizens speculated that he was responsible for starting it.*

a mud-wrestling contest, and the conservative Romans were shocked and outraged. When a plot to assassinate Nero and replace him with Gaius Calpurnius Piso was uncovered, among the conspirators forced to commit suicide were Nero's old mentor Seneca and the poet Lucan.

In AD 67, with Rome in crisis, Nero left for an extravagant tour of Greece. Increasingly paranoid, he ordered the popular and successful general Gnaeus Domitius Corbulo to commit suicide. Fearing for their own lives, the governors of the Roman provinces went into open revolt.

The legions proclaimed Servius Supoicius Galba, the governor of Spain, emperor. The Senate then condemned Nero to die a slave's death, being whipped and crucified. When his Praetorian Guard turned against him, Nero fled. There are two versions of his death. In one, told by Suetonius, he stabbed himself in the throat with a dagger on 9 June AD 68. Tacitus, on the other hand, records that Nero reached the Greek islands in the guise of a red-haired prophet and leader of the poor. The governor of Cythnos had him arrested in AD 69 and carried out the sentence passed by the Senate. Whichever version is correct, it seems clear that Nero met a premature end as a direct result of his tyranny; he would not, however, be the last tyrant to hold power in Rome.

# Life and Crimes

AD 37   Born 15 December at Antrium, modern-day Anzio, Italy.

AD 54   Proclaimed emperor, but the real power stayed with his mother as regent.

AD 59   Murders his mother.

AD 62   Begins treason trials to purge enemies.

AD 64   Rome burns down while, some say, Nero fiddled; builds lavish palace and begins persecution of the Christians.

AD 67   Begins extravagant tour of Greece, leaving a freedman in charge in Rome; forces Corbulo to commit suicide.

# Attila the Hun

◀ c. 406–453 ▶

## KING OF THE HUNS

The aggressive and ambitious chieftain of the nomadic Huns was known in his own time as 'the scourge of God' for his savagery. Little is known of his early life, but in 434 he and his brother Bleda inherited an empire that stretched from the Alps to the Baltic from their uncle Ruga, who already had a treaty with Rome. Attila and Bleda renewed the treaty, in the process upping the tribute Rome had to pay for peace to 700 pounds of gold a year.

The Huns turned their attention east, expanding their conquests into Scythia, Media and Persia. But when in 439 the eastern emperor failed to pay his tribute Attila attacked, razing Singidunum – Belgrade – and other Balkan cities. A truce allowed the Romans to regroup, but in 443 Attila went on to destroy Naissus (Nis in Serbia) and Serdica (Sofia in Bulgaria). The Huns reached the walls of Constantinople and defeated the Romans in the east. Emperor Theodosius II was forced to pay the arrears of 6,000 pounds of gold, plus a tribute of 2,100 pounds a year from then on.

In 445 Attila assassinated his brother and made himself sole leader. He devastated the Balkans again in 447. He drove southwards into Greece, only to be stopped at Thermopylae. One chronicler said: 'There was so much killing and bloodletting that no one could number the dead. The Huns pillaged the churches and monasteries, and slew the monks and virgins... They so devastated Thrace that it will never rise again.'

A new treaty was concluded with the Eastern Empire in 449, ceding territory to the Huns. Then Attila turned his attention to the Western Empire. His excuse for breaking their treaty was that Honoria, the sister of the Emperor Valentinian, had sent him a ring. She had been having an affair with her steward, who had been executed. Pregnant, she begged the King of the Huns to rescue her. But he pretended that the ring was an offer of marriage and asked for half of the Western Empire as a dowry.

In the spring of 451, Attila forged an alliance with the Franks and Vandals and unleashed an attack on the heart of western Europe. In April

*Atilla the Hun unleashed a wave of devastation on the late Roman Empire.*

he took Metz with an army of between 300,000 and 700,000. Rheims, Mainz, Strasbourg, Cologne, Worms and Trier were destroyed. He was besieging Orleans, when a Roman army under Flavius Aetius, supported by forces under the Visigothic king Theodoric I, arrived. In the bloody battle of Catalaunian, Theodoric was killed, but Flavius dealt Attila his one and only defeat.

Instead of retreating, he gathered his forces and invaded Italy the following year, sacking Aquilean, Milan, Padua, Verona, Brescia and Bergamo. The survivors fled to a group of defensible islands in the Adriatic and founded Venice. It is said that Attila turned back before the gates of Rome because he was so impressed by the holiness of Pope Leo I, who came out of the city to parley. In fact, there was disease and famine in the area at the time and he may have feared the return of the Roman legions who had been fighting abroad.

With their booty the Huns turned back to the north. Along the way the 47-year-old Attila took a new wife, named Ildico. After drinking heavily on his wedding day, he went to bed with his young bride. The next morning, he was found dead, drowned in the blood from a nosebleed.

# Life and Crimes

**c. 406** Born.

**434** Becomes joint king of the Huns with brother Bleda.

**439** Attacks Eastern Roman Empire.

**443** Destroys Belgrade, Nis and Sofia; takes Philippolis; destroys Roman forces in the east.

**445** Murders his brother.

**447** Attacks Eastern Empire again.

**449** Secures treaty with Constantinople.

**451** Invades Gaul; defeated by Flavius Aetius in battle of the Catalaunian Plains.

**452** Invades Italy; sacks northern cities.

**453** Dies in his sleep on his wedding night.

# THE MIDDLE AGES

By the Medieval period, communications were improving and Europeans got to learn more about tyrants as far away as India, Mongolia, Central Asia, China and Japan. Indeed Genghis Khan's Golden Horde brought tyranny to the gates of Europe with incursions into Russia, Georgia and the Ukraine. Following in his footsteps was Tamerlane. There were still many home-grown tyrants in Europe. Meanwhile Spain began exporting tyranny with the excesses of Hermán Cortés and Francisco Pizarro in the Americas, ruthlessly destroying the civilizations that flourished there. With the development of modern means of travel, weaponry and systems of government, tyranny had become a truly global phenomenon.

# Wu Zetian

◀ 625–705 ▶

## EMPRESS OF CHINA

Born under the name Wu Chao, she entered service as a junior concubine to the first Tang emperor of China, T'ai Tsung, at the age of 13. On his death in 649, she transferred her affections to his heir Kao Tsung, becoming his favourite wife. She murdered his other concubines and wives – including the then empress – becoming empress herself in 655, when she became known as 'Wu Hou' (Empress Wu).

Wu Chao then began to exert influence in government, eliminating those who complained that her relationship with the emperor was incestuous. Numerous elder statesmen – including the emperor's uncle – were executed or exiled. By 660, with the emperor ailing, she was in complete command. She hired and fired government ministers and hand-picked the military commanders who invaded Korea on her orders in 660 and 668.

When Kao Tsung died in 683, Wu Hou's son Chung Tsung succeeded. Within a month, she had deposed and exiled him, placing on the throne her second son Jui Tsung but ruling herself as regent. A revolt in favour of Chung Tsung was crushed.

In 690, she usurped the throne herself, ruling for the next fifteen years under the regnal name 'Wu Zetian'. However, two depraved courtiers, the Chang brothers, gained favour, outraging government ministers and generals. In 705, there was a coup at the palace, and the Changs were executed; the empress was forced to hand power to her son Chung Tsung. At the age of 80, she retired to her summer palace, dying soon after.

# Life and Crimes

**625** Born daughter of senior government official.

**638** Becomes junior concubine to T'ai Tsung.

**649** Becomes favourite wife of Kao Tsung.

**655** Becomes empress after murdering rivals.

**660** Rules unopposed after purging government of enemies.

**683** Deposes first son; installs second son and rules as regent.

**690** Takes throne in own right.

**699** Favours depraved Chang brothers.

**705** Retires after palace revolution; dies 16 December.

# Harun al-Rashid

## ◄ 763–809 ►

## CALIPH OF BAGHDAD

Harun al-Rashid was known as a generous man before he came to power as Caliph of Baghdad in 786. He then became a fanatical follower of cock and dog fighting. A notorious insomniac, he would stalk the streets at night in disguise with an executioner, just in case he wanted to order the death of someone he met.

Harun had been brought up by Yahya Barmakid, who became his chief minister. But Harun fell out with Yahya's son Jafar, his best friend, possibly due to homosexual jealousy. It is also said that Harun had arranged for Jafar to marry his sister secretly, provided he did not consummate the marriage. When they fell in love and had a child, Harun ordered that the entire Barmakid family be killed, along with his sister and her children.

After attacking the Byzantine Empire, Harun turned east to put down a revolt in Iran. During the campaign, he grew ill. The captured brother of the rebel chief was brought to his deathbed and Harun's last words were reportedly: 'If I had no more breath in my life but to say a single word, it would be, "slay him".'

Harun has however remained very popular in the Arab world, mostly for his establishment of Baghdad as a major world city, and many of the stories contained in *One Thousand and One Nights* concern him.

## Life and Crimes

**763** Born in March in Rayy, Iran.
**786** Succeeds father as caliph after brother dies, possibly at the hand of his mother.
**803** Wipes out the Barmakids.
**809** Dies 24 March at Tus.

# Genghis Khan
━◀ c. 1162–1227 ▶━
## RULER OF THE MONGOLS

'I have committed many acts of cruelty and had an incalculable number of men killed, never knowing whether what I did was right. But I am indifferent to what people think of me.' So said Genghis Khan in the thirteenth century. By the time he died in 1227, he had been responsible for the death of around 20 million people, around one-tenth of the population of the known world at that time.

The 'tyrant's tyrant', Genghis began his murderous career at the age of 12 when he killed his brother in a dispute over a fish. By the age of 33, he had risen to become the undisputed leader of the Mongol hordes – taking the name Genghis Khan, which means 'universal ruler'. In 1211, he began his conquest of imperial China, burning and pillaging every town and village on the way.

In 1212 Shah Mohammed staged a coup d'état to become ruler of the neighbouring Muslim empire of Khwarezam, covering Iran, Afghanistan, Turkmeniya, Uzbekistan and Tadjikstan. Eager to maintain good relations with Khwarezam, Genghis sent a caravan to the Shah carrying exquisite jade, ivory, gold bars and felt made from perfect white camel hair. The 300 caravaners were accompanied by a Mongolian noble who carried a message from the Khan. It read: 'I know your power and the vast extent of your empire. I have the greatest desire to live in peace with you. I shall regard you as my son. For your part, you must know that I have conquered the Middle Kingdom and subdued all the tribes of the north. You know that my country is a swarm of warriors, a mine of silver, and that I have no need to covet further domains. We have equal interest in encouraging trade between our subjects.'

The Shah was a little suspicious of this message. He accepted the Khan's gifts but sent his messenger back without a reply. Genghis sent a second caravan, this time consisting of 500 camels, laden with the fur of beaver and sable. With it was Uquna, an official of the Mongolian court.

At the frontier town of Otrar, the local governor had 100 of the caravanners – including Uquna – butchered and their cargo confiscated. Genghis had one more go at diplomacy. He sent a new emissary, this time a Muslim. The Shah had him put to death and his entourage returned with their heads shaven. As a final insult to the Khan, he confirmed the murderous governor of Otrar in office.

There could be only one response. In the summer of 1219, Genghis Khan assembled between 150,000 and 200,000 horsemen. Many were battle-hardened veterans of the conquest of China. Together with his horsemen, his best generals, his four sons and one of his wives – Qulan, which means 'she-ass' – Genghis Khan set off to make war.

Shah Mohammed's army easily outnumbered Genghis Khan's. But he did not know where the Mongols were going to attack so he deployed his men all along the border, a classic military blunder. Mohammed's men were so thinly spread that wherever the Mongols attacked they were bound to win. If the Shah had thought about it for a moment, he would have known where Genghis Khan was going to attack – at Otrar, of course, where the governor had killed his emissary.

Using siege engines captured from the Chinese, and also the Chinese expertise in gunpowder, the walled city of Otrar was soon captured and the unfortunate inhabitants subject to the usual horrors, including the governor, who was executed by having molten silver poured into his ears and eye sockets.

The cities of Khwarezam continued to fall to Genghis's troops, and the Mongols soon reached the holy city of Bukhara, famed for its carpet weaving. When the Mongols attacked, the Turkish garrison tried to break out. They were hunted down and slaughtered. The Mongol prisoners were sent to break the gates down and catapults shattered the defences. Genghis Khan entered the city personally while fighting was still going on in the citadel. When it was captured, the last of the defenders were put to death. The inhabitants were lined up and told to leave. Anyone remaining in the city was stabbed to death.

Genghis Khan himself rode into the great mosque, believing it to be the Shah's palace. Sacred Koranic books were thrown in the dirt. Hundreds of devout Muslims killed themselves rather than submit to the barbaric invaders. Men killed their wives rather than let the Mongols take them:

the Mongols had a practice of making men watch while they raped their womenfolk. Among those who died by their own hand was the Imam of the Great Mosque.

'It was an appalling day,' says a Muslim historian. 'Nothing was heard but the sobbing of men, women and children, separated forever as the Mongol troops parcelled the population among themselves.'

To Genghis Khan were attributed the words: 'I tell you I am the scourge of Allah, and if you had not been great sinners Allah would not have brought down my wrath upon your heads.'

The city was then burnt to the ground. For dozens of years afterwards Bukhara lay uninhabited. Thousands of corpses, too many to be buried, exuded diseases and those who lived in the surrounding region moved away. The irrigation ditches collapsed. The fields turned to desert and the animals, left to their own devices, perished. All that was left were the ruins.

Genghis Khan then turned on Samarkand. Behind him trudged a swelling army of prisoners, forced to work as slave labourers to destroy their own country. Samarkand was a city steeped in history. It had been ancient when Alexander the Great had conquered it in 329 BC. Now it was one of the foremost trading centres in the world. It sent melons as far as Baghdad, packed in lead boxes lined with snow to keep them fresh. It boasted goldsmiths, silversmiths, coppersmiths, tanners, saddle-makers, wood carvers, cabinet makers and swordsmiths. Chain mail, carved ewers, ceramics and beautifully inlaid woodwork made there were traded in the ports of the Mediterranean. They even made paper in the city, using a technique imported from China.

Samarkand had recently been fortified. In the ramparts there were four great gates, symbolizing the city's dependence on trade. It had a huge garrison, manned largely by Turkish mercenaries, and few of the inhabitants thought that it would suffer the same fate as Bukhara.

Genghis Khan was impressed by the defences too. When he arrived in the spring of 1220, he camped outside the city and waited for reinforcements. Meanwhile, he deployed a curtain of troops round the city. When two of his sons turned up with thousands of prisoners, they decided the best ploy was to impress the enemy with their numbers. They took the prisoners' clothes from them and dressed them as Mongols.

*A prisoner of the Mongols is flogged, watched by Genghis himself.*

Then, under close guard and with Mongol banners flying, they marched them towards the city walls.

The city's garrison charged the attackers. The Mongols turned and fled, leaving the unarmed prisoners to absorb the assault, then they turned and counter-attacked, hacking through the Turkish mercenaries. The survivors deserted, leaving the city defenceless.

The town's leaders came out to talk to the Mongols. Genghis Khan promised that all those who left the city would be spared. Some 50,000 citizens bought their freedom with a ransom that totalled 200,000 dinars. Those too poor to pay the ransom were taken as slave labourers by the Mongol units. Craftsmen were sent to Mongolia. Anyone who stayed behind was butchered. Once the city was empty, Samarkand was sacked. Part of the city was set on fire. Genghis Khan considered the Turkish mercenaries criminals and killed any he caught up with. One Persian chronicler says 30,000 were massacred. It was said that when those who had paid the ransom returned to Samarkand there were so few of them they could only repopulate a quarter of the city.

The capital of Khwarezam was not Samarkand but Urgench, 300 miles up the Amudar'ya River towards the Aral Sea. Again it was defended by Turkish mercenaries. But this time they were ready. They carefully stockpiled weapons, food and water, ready for a long siege.

Genghis Khan charged three of his sons to take Urgench, naming one of them, Jochi, ruler of Khwarezam, so it was in his interests not to destroy the city completely. With them were three of the Khan's most experienced generals, and 50,000 horsemen.

An emissary was sent demanding unconditional surrender. The offer was declined and the Mongols laid siege to the city. There were no boulders in the area for the catapults, so prisoners were sent out to find mulberry trees and their trunks were sawn up to make ammunition. Meanwhile other prisoners, under fire from the city walls, began filling in the moat. It took 12 days. That done, sappers advanced under the cover of siege engines and started chipping away at the brickwork.

Soon after, the walls were breached. But, aware of what would happen to them if they were defeated, the defenders fought ferociously, house to house. Both sides used burning naphtha to set fire to houses where their foes took shelter, with a consequently high loss of life for the civilian inhabitants.

The Mongols were used to fighting huge sweeping battles. This sort of fighting did not suit them and they paid a heavy price. Having taken one half of the city, they attacked the bridge over the Amudar'ya River that led to the other half and were repulsed. This action alone cost them 3,000 men.

The Turkish mercenaries continued their stout defence from the ruins of the city, supported and supplied by the remaining inhabitants. After seven days, the Mongols lost their patience and torched the rest of the city. The Turks were forced to pull back but hundreds of civilians were burnt to death. Eventually, members of the city council indicated that they wanted to parley. One begged the Mongols to have mercy on the brave men who had defended the city.

'We have seen the might of your wrath; now show us the measure of your pity,' he said.

But the Mongols were in no mood for this kind of talk and the fighting continued.

'Everyone fought,' wrote an Arab historian, 'men, women and children, and they went on fighting until the Mongols had taken the entire town, killed all the inhabitants, and pillaged everything there was to be found. Then they opened the dam and the waters of the river flooded the city and destroyed it completely... Those who escaped from the massacre were drowned or buried under the rubble. And then nothing remained but ruins and waves.'

Genghis Khan was not at all happy about the destruction of Shah Mohammed's capital. The siege of Urgench had lasted six months, with much higher Mongolian losses than he was used to. His sons further incurred his wrath by seizing all the booty from what little remained of the city, leaving nothing for their father.

Meanwhile, the Khan's generals pursued Shah Mohammed whose troops deserted in droves. City after city fell to the Mongols until the whole of Khwarezam was in their hands. Shah Mohammed died of pleurisy on the shores of the Caspian Sea, in what is now Azerbaijan.

Genghis Khan took a summer break at the oasis of Nasaf. Then he went north to Termez. When the city refused to surrender, he laid siege to it for seven days. When it fell, the usual massacre ensued, the entire populace being disembowelled after one woman swallowed her pearls rather than hand them over.

Next he headed for the ancient city of Balkh, capital of the kingdom of Bactria in what is now northern Afghanistan. As a city, it had been known for 3,000 years. Alexander the Great had occupied it and married his Princess Roxane there. But when the city surrendered to Genghis Khan on the understanding that its citizens would go unmolested, he went back on his promise and put thousands to the sword. When he passed that way again in 1222, he massacred the survivors. A Chinese monk travelling through the region at the time reported that the great city of Balkh was a ghost town with dogs barking in the street.

'Wherever there was a wall still standing, the Mongols tore it down,' said an Arab historian, 'and for a second time swept away all traces of civilization from the region.'

Genghis Khan spared some cities, but if there was the slightest sign of opposition, he was merciless. As well as massacring the inhabitants, he would destroy the irrigation systems that had taken centuries to construct. Many cities that the Mongols ravaged were destroyed forever.

In February 1221, Genghis Khan's fourth son, Tolui, and 70,000 horsemen arrived at Merv, now called Mary, in Turkmeniya. It was a rich city famed for its ceramics. Its fortifications were particularly impressive. Tolui and 500 horsemen spent all day inspecting them. Twice he assaulted the city and was driven back. But the governor then surrendered, having received assurances that no one would come to harm.

Tolui did not keep his word. He evacuated the city and picked out 400 craftsmen and some children to keep as slaves. The rest were put to the sword. This was a formidable task. The population had to be divided up among the army units. Each man, it was said, had to kill 300–400 people. One source says that Tolui left 700,000 corpses there. Another said he stopped counting after 1,300,000.

In Herat, after a siege that lasted eight days, only the mercenaries were massacred. But later, the populace revolted, killing the Mongol governor and the Khan's resident minister. In revenge, the Mongols slaughtered the population, then withdrew and waited. When survivors emerged from the rubble and those who had taken refuge in nearby caves returned, the Mongols went back and killed them too. One source says there were 1.3 million dead, another 2.4 million.

'Not a man, not an ear of corn; no scrap of food, not an item of clothing remained,' it was said.

Mongol contingents were also sent back to Merv and Balkh to slaughter anyone who had returned to the cities they had laid waste. Next on the list was Bamiyan, where huge Buddhas were carved in the rocks (the Buddhas survived Genghis, only to be destroyed by the Afghani Taleban in 2002). It was the jewel of Khwarezam, a stop-off on the Silk Route and an unparalleled centre of culture. The story goes that the city was betrayed by Princess Lala Qatun, whose father was trying to marry her off against her will. She sent word to Genghis telling him how the city's water supply could be turned off.

However, during the siege, Genghis's grandson was killed. Genghis was so angered by the loss of his grandson that he did not even stop to put his helmet on before he started slaughtering the enemy. The boy's father was away at the time. When he returned, the Khan rebuked his son falsely for having disobeyed him and asked his son whether he was now ready to obey any order his father gave him. His son swore he was.

'Well,' said Genghis, 'your son has been killed and I order you not to lament.'

The entire population, predictably, was then massacred. Even Princess Lala Qatun was not spared: she was stoned to death for her treachery.

After the death of Shah Mohammed, power passed to his son Prince Jalal a-Din. With an army composed of Turkish mercenaries and Khwarezamian conscripts numbering around 60,000, he holed up in a fortress at Ghazi, 100 miles south of Kabul. The Mongols attacked but, after losing 1,000 men, were forced to withdraw.

The Khan's adopted brother was in charge of the assault. Short of men, he thought he would fool Prince Jalal into believing he had more men than he had. He mounted straw dummies on horseback and rode them up to his camp as if they were a relief army. The ruse did not work. The Prince attacked. For the first time on Muslim territory, the Mongols suffered a defeat. The Muslim soldiers were said to have surpassed even the Mongols in their savagery, driving nails into the ears of their prisoners.

When Genghis Khan heard of this, he leapt into the saddle. With fresh troops, he rode continuously for two days to reach Ghazi. The story goes that they did not even stop to eat or drink, but rather – in the Mongol way – cut a nick in the back of their horse's neck each time they felt peckish and nourished themselves with blood.

By the time they reached Ghazi, a dispute had broken out between the Turkish mercenaries and the local troops and Prince Jalal was forced to withdraw. The city's inhabitants were deported or killed and its defences destroyed.

The Prince planned to escape to the Punjab but was caught with his back to the river Indus. There he surrounded himself with a square of troops and made a stand. But the Mongols steadily hacked away at his lines of defence. When he had only a handful of men left, the Prince made a break for it and jumped off a cliff on horseback into the river. Genghis Khan was full of admiration – first for how the Prince had saved his own life at the expense of those of his men, and then for the leap. He was an example to all Mongols, the Khan said, and was allowed to escape. The men who had made the jump with the Prince were not accorded the same respect. Mongol archers rained arrows down on them in the water. Prince Jalal eventually found refuge with the Sultan of Delhi.

Genghis Khan made only a brief incursion into India. He laid waste to a few villages around Lahore, but then turned back into Khwarezam to take a closer look at the land he had already conquered.

Meanwhile, following the death of Shah Mohammed, the Khan's general Jebe had moved on northwards into Georgia, defeating the Georgian cavalry, the mightiest in the region. Then he moved on into Russia.

At the battle of Kalka, the Mongols were attacked by 80,000 knights under Prince Mstislav. The Mongols, numbering only 20,000, used their tried and tested tactic. After a short engagement, they withdrew, apparently in disorder. The Russians pursed them at high speed. This stretched out their army. Then, when they outnumbered the advance guard, the Mongols turned and fought. When the rest of the army arrived, they would come upon a scene of appalling butchery, which usually put them off fighting. If not, the Mongols slaughtered them as well.

The Russian knights wore steel armour and had shields, axes, swords and lances, but were heavy and slow compared to the Mongol horsemen and they were easy prey for Mongolian archers. They were easily defeated and Prince Mstislav was captured. He was executed by being wrapped up in a carpet and suffocated. As a mark of respect, the Mongols would not shed his blood.

The rest of the Russian army were intimidated by Mstislav's defeat and withdrew. The Mongols went on to plunder the warehouses of Sudak in the Crimea. They looted the kingdom of the Bulgars, then they turned for home cutting a swathe through Kazakhstan.

Genghis Khan himself returned to Mongolia and died on the shores of Lake Baikal in 1227. He left orders that, if anyone gazed on his coffin, the next coffin would be theirs.

In 1237, ten years after the death of Genghis Khan, the Mongolian 'Golden Horde' attacked Russia again, employing similar barbarous tactics. In 1347, during the Siege of Caffa on the Crimea, they invented biological warfare, catapulting the corpses of plague victims over the walls to infect those within. The Mongols continued to plague the Russians for centuries. As a traditional Russian tale 'The Story of the Destruction of Ryazan' puts it: 'They devastated the churches of God and before the consecrated altars they spilt quantities of blood. And none was spared, all perished equally and drank the cup of death to the lees. No one remained to sob or weep for the dead – neither father or mother for their children, nor children for their father and mother, neither brother for brother, nor cousin for cousin – for all without exception lay lifeless. And this happened in requital of our sins.'

## Life and Crimes

**1162** Born (though some sources give 1165 or 1167 as his date of birth).

**1195** Becomes leader of the Mongols.

**1211** Begins conquest of Imperial China.

**1217** Returns to Mongolia victorious with five hundred slaves.

**1220** Massacres 30,000 in Samarkand; massacres citizens of Balkh; kills 70,000 at Nessa.

**1221** Four hundred slaves taken at Merv, the rest of the inhabitants put to death; populations of Neyshabur and Herat slaughtered.

**1222** Massacres anyone who has returned to Balkh or Merv; population of Bamiyan slaughtered.

**1223** Slaughters Russian knights at the battle of Kalka; loots Sudak, the kingdom of the Bulgars and Kazakhstan.

**1227** Dies on the shores of Lake Baikal.

# Pedro the Cruel

## ◄ 1334–1369 ►

## KING OF CASTILE

Pedro was just fifteen when he came to the throne of Castile. Although he was in love with the beautiful María de Padilla, he married Blanche, daughter of the Duke of Bourbon, to seal an alliance with France. However, he immediately abandoned Blanche – some say he murdered her – and took up with María who remained his mistress until her death in 1361. Queen Blanche died the same year, but Pedro claimed that María was actually his legitimate wife having married her in secret first.

Pedro had had a troubled upbringing. After he had been born, his father Alfonso XI of Castile spurned his mother María of Portugal and went on to have ten children with his mistress Eleanor of Guzmán. He inaugurated his reign by killing a supporter of his half-brothers. He also had his father's mistress killed. On the eve of his execution, one of his former ministers wrote to the young king pleading, 'Now at the moment of death, I give you my final counsel – if you do not put aside the dagger, if you do not stop committing such murders, then you shall lose your realm and place your person in the greatest jeopardy.'

As rivals for the throne, his four half-brothers turned against him. He put down the insurrection ruthlessly, killing three of them. One, Henry, escaped to France. With the backing of Charles V of France, Pope Urban V and Peter IV of Aragon, Henry expelled Pedro with an army of mercenaries. Pedro then sought the backing of Edward, the Black Prince, who helped him take back his throne.

Henry raised a second army in France, defeated and captured Pedro, whom he murdered on 23 March 1369. It was part of Henry's propaganda offensive to stick Pedro with the epithet 'the Cruel'; others have called him Pedro the Just. He also dubbed Pedro 'King of Jews', stirring up anti-Semitic sentiment in Castile. Pedro responded by having at least five of the leaders of anti-Jewish riots executed by boiling and roasting.

# Life and Crimes

**1334**  Born in Castile.

**1350**  Succeeds his father to the throne.

**1352**  Marries Blanche of France; abandons – or murders – her.

**1356**  Kills three brothers; Henry flees to France to raise army and oust Pedro.

**1367**  With help of Edward, the Black Prince, Pedro retakes throne.

**1369**  Murdered by Henry 23 March 1969.

# Tamerlane

## ◄ 1336–1405 ►

## RULER OF SAMARKAND

A Muslim of Turkic origins, Tamerlane took the motto of all true tyrants: 'As there is but one God in heaven,' he said, 'there ought to be but one ruler on the earth'.

Born in Kesh, near Samarkand in 1336 into a minor military family, he was named Timur. However, he was injured by an arrow-wound while stealing sheep which left him partially paralysed down his left-hand side, making him 'Timur the Lame' or 'Tamerlane'. He rose to become chief minister of his local region Transoxania – modern Uzbekistan – under the governor Ilyas Khoja in 1361. He soon rebelled to join his brother-in-law Amir Husayn, however, and together they defeated Ilyas Khoja in 1364 and completed their conquest of Transoxania by 1366.

In 1370, he turned against Husayn and killed him. Making himself ruler in Samarkand, he claimed sovereignty over the Mongols. Declaring himself a direct descendant of Genghis Khan, he set out to restore his lost empire with an army of 100,000 horsemen, armed with bows and swords, and carrying all they needed on their own pack animals.

Over the next ten years, he occupied Turkistan and sent troops into Russia in support of Tokhamysh, the Mongol Khan of the Crimea. They occupied Moscow and crushed the Lithuanians.

In 1383, Tamerlane turned his attention to Persia, completing his conquest in 1385. Seventy thousand people were killed at Isfahan alone when he butchered the inhabitants of the city. Over the next eight years, he conquered Iraq and Central Asia. In 1391, he defeated Tokhamysh and his Golden Horde on the Russian steppes, defeating him again on the River Kur and occupying Moscow in 1395. Meanwhile, Persia had revolted. He returned to put down the uprising with unbridled savagery, massacring entire cities and building pyramids of the inhabitants' skulls.

On 24 September 1398, he crossed the Indus on the pretext that the Muslim rulers of Delhi were treating their Hindu subjects with unnecessary tolerance. Victorious at the battle of Panipat on 17 December

1398, he ordered the slaughter of 100,000 captured Indian soldiers. He then massacred the inhabitants of Delhi, stripped the city and destroyed everything his men could not carry. It would be over a century before Delhi fully recovered.

While he was in India, the Mameluke sultan of Egypt and the Ottoman sultan Bayezid I had encroached on his territory. He set out to punish them in 1399. In 1401 he defeated the Mameluke army in Syria, slaughtering the inhabitants of Damascus. In Baghdad, 20,000 were massacred and the city's monuments levelled. The following year he defeated the Ottoman army near Ankara and extended his empire to the Mediterranean, taking Smyrna – modern Izmir – from the kings of Rhodes. Bayezid was captured and died in captivity in 1403.

In December 1404 at the age of 68 Tamerlane set off again to conquer China. But in February 1405 he fell ill and died in Otrar, near Chimkent – modern Shymkent in Kazakhstan. His body was embalmed and taken back to Samarkand.

*Tamerlane established a fearsome reputation, putting the inhabitants of conquered cities to the sword and then building pyramids out of their skulls.*

# Life and Crimes

**1336** Born at Kesh near Samarkand.

**1366** Conquers Transoxania.

**1370** Becomes ruler of Samarkand; declares himself descendant of Genghis Khan.

**1380** Subdues Turkistan.

**1383** Takes Herat, Persia.

**1385** Completes conquest of Persia.

**1387** Kills 70,000 inhabitants of Isfahan, and constructs a pyramid of their severed heads outside the city walls.

**1391** Invades Russia.

**1394** Completes conquest of Iraq and Central Asia.

**1395** Occupies Moscow.

**1396** Subdues revolt in Persia.

**1398** Invades India; destroys Delhi.

**1401** Defeats Mamelukes; occupies Damascus; destroys Baghdad.

**1402** Defeats the Ottomans.

**1404** Sets out to invade China.

**1405** Dies 19 February.

# Tomas de Torquemada
## ◀ 1420–1498 ▶
### GRAND INQUISITOR OF SPAIN

Dominican friar Tomas de Torquemada persuaded King Ferdinand of Aragon and Queen Isabella of Castile to set up the Spanish Inquisition, which tortured and killed in the name of the Catholic Church.

Born at Valladolid in Castile in 1420, he was a nephew of the celebrated theologian and cardinal, Juan de Torquemada. In his early youth he entered the Dominican monastery at Valladolid, and later was appointed prior of the Monastery of Santa Cruz at Segovia, an office he held for twenty-two years. The Infanta Isabella chose him as her confessor while at Segovia. When she succeeded to the throne of Castile in 1474 he became one of her most trusted and influential councillors, but refused all high ecclesiastical preferments and chose to remain a simple friar. He prided himself on living an extremely austere life: he did not eat meat and, unlike other Dominicans, he refused to wear linen under his coarse habit. If that was not chafing enough, he often resorted to wearing a hair shirt. And he always went barefoot.

In 1483 he became Grand Inquisitor, first of Castile then of Aragon. He wrote the twenty-eight articles which helped his inquisitors root out sorcery, bigamy, sodomy and usury as well as heresy, blasphemy and apostasy. And he authorized the use of torture – up to and including the point of death – to extract a confession. Although of Jewish extraction himself, he persuaded Ferdinand and Isabella to expel all Jews from Spain and spent much of his time persecuting Jews who had converted to Christianity. In 1490, Torquemada staged a show trial of eight Jews accused of the ritual murder of a Christian child, a common libel levelled at the Jews in the Middle Ages. Although no evidence was offered against the accused, and no body was found, they were found guilty and burnt at the stake. Torquemada used this to argue that the Jews were a threat to Spain, and on 31 March 1492 he persuaded Ferdinand and Isabella to issue the Edict of Expulsion. Torquemada enthusiastically administered this edict, which saw mediaeval Europe's largest population of Jews made refugees. Any that remained in Spain were burnt.

Under Torquemada, the Spanish Inquisition operated very differently from that in Germany or France in that it travelled around the country, actively seeking out victims, and there was no hiding place from the Inquisition. If a count or a duke refused to let the Inquisition into his realm, he would be found guilty of aiding and abetting heresy.

Torquemada took a broad definition of heresy. Besides being a witch or a Jew, bigamy also qualified, as marriage was a sacrament. Sodomy was also punished by burning. Officers of the Inquisition were not allowed to take gifts from suspects. If they did, they would have to forfeit twice the value of the gift and might suffer excommunication – putting paid to a lucrative career in the Church. Torquemada also reserved the right to sack inquisitors for other misdemeanours, such as not being harsh enough.

Torture was Torquemada's great contribution to the Inquisition. He gave orders that it should be used in any case where heresy was 'half proven' – that is, an accusation had been laid but no confession had been extracted. Simply being brought before the Inquisition was enough. Being a good Christian, Torquemada said that no blood must be shed and his inquisitors usually avoided breaking the skin. However, he conceded that people did die under torture. If this happened, the inquisitor must immediately seek absolution from a fellow priest. Torquemada gave all his priests the power to absolve one another of murder.

The word torture was not used. Prisoners were simply put to 'The Question'. There were five carefully thought out stages to The Question. The first was the threat. The prisoner would already have heard about the cruel methods that the Inquisition used, but the inquisitors outlined the appalling tortures the victim faced, in the hope that fear alone would force a confession.

The second step was the journey to the torture chamber. The victim would be taken in a procession by candle light. The torture chamber would be dark and dismal, lit only by braziers which would have their own terrifying significance. The victims would be given a little time to look around and see the hideous devices that were employed. They would see other victims being tortured, and they would be introduced to the torturers who wore black hoods with eyeholes cut in them.

In the third stage, the prisoner would be stripped, leaving them naked and vulnerable. The fourth stage was to introduce the victim to the particular instrument that was to be used on them. Only then, in the fifth and final stage, would the pain begin.

It was technically against the law to repeat The Question. Once a victim had been tortured and survived, they could not be tortured again. However, the torture could continue day after day, week after week, with any interval merely being a 'suspension'.

Although the rack was used by the Inquisition, most prisoners were subjected to the strappado and squassation. With the strappado, the victim's hands were tied behind them. The bond was then attached to a rope and they were hauled up to the ceiling and left dangling there. In squassation, the victim was hauled up in the strappado, then dropped, their fall being jerked to a halt inches short of the floor.

If that did not work, water torture was used. The accused would be tied to a sloping trestle so their feet were higher than their head, which was held in place with a band of metal. The nostrils would be sealed with wooden pegs and their jaw opened with a piece of iron. A piece of linen would be put over their mouth and water would be poured down their throat, carrying the linen with it. The victim would swallow automatically, pulling the linen into the gullet. They would cough and retch and reach a state of semi-suffocation. When they struggled the ropes would cut into them. More and more water would be brought, with up to eight jars used on occasion.

Another favourite of the men in hoods was the Spanish Chair. This was an iron chair with metal bands that held the victim so they could not move. Their bare feet would be put in stocks next to a brazier, then covered in fat and slowly allowed to roast. Fat was applied so that the flesh did not burn away too quickly. Sometimes the victim had to be taken to the auto-da-fé in the chair because their feet had been completely burnt away. Flogging was also common practice, as was the amputation of fingers and toes, as well as other more imaginative tortures.

Legally, confessions extracted under torture were not valid. So twenty-four hours later, the victim was taken back to the Holy Office, where their confession was read out. Under oath they had to swear that it was correct in every detail. If they did not, the torture, which had merely been suspended, would be resumed. Otherwise the victim would be sent to the auto-da-fé.

Auto-da-fé means 'act of faith' and these public executions took place on Sundays or other holy days to allow more people the chance to watch.

The victims were taken to the quemadero – the place of burning – and tied to stakes. They were asked if they wanted absolution. The lucky ones were garrotted, then the faggots around their feet were lit. Monks chanted, people cheered, and the inquisitors feigned shock at the wickedness of the world.

During Torquemada's term of office as Grand Inquisitor, over two thousand heretics were killed in this way. His persecutions were so ruthless that Pope Alexander VI – of all people – appointed four assistant inquisitors to restrain him. Although ill health forced him to retire in 1494, he continued to oversee the activities of the Inquisition from his monastery in Avila until 1498, when he died peacefully in his bed. He had lived to see the Muslims forced out of Granada as well as the expulsion of the Jews. At the time many people called him the 'Saviour of Spain'.

Even after Torquemada's death, his Inquisition continued its grim work. It tortured and burnt victims in Spain for the next two hundred years and it burnt its last victim in the New World in 1836.

## Life and Crimes

**1420**   Born in Valladolid, Spain.

**1452**   Becomes prior of the Monastery of Santa Cruz in Segovia.

**1478**   Persuades Ferdinand and Isabella to set up Spanish Inquisition.

**1483**   Becomes Grand Inquisitor.

**1484**   Issues 28 articles for the guidance of inquisitors.

**1492**   Expels Jews from Spain.

**1494**   Pope appoints assistant inquisitors to restrain him; retires due to ill health.

**1498**   Dies 16 September in Avila, Castile.

# Vlad the Impaler
◀ c. 1431–1476 ▶
## COUNT OF WALLACHIA

The inspiration for Bram Stoker's Count Dracula, Vlad Tepes became ruler of Wallachia, directly to the south of Transylvania, in 1456. He did not drink blood but he did have at least 50,000 people – about one-tenth of the population of Wallachia – put to death.

Descended from Basarb the Great, the fourteenth-century founder of the state of Wallachia, Vlad's father was honoured by the Holy Roman Emperor Sigismund with membership of the Order of the Dragon – or Dracul in Wallachian. This meant his son was 'son of a dragon' or Dracula.

Vlad was educated in the Wallachian court but, when Sigismund died, Vlad's father made a deal with the Turkish sultan to guarantee Wallachia's independence. Under this, the eleven-year-old Vlad and his six-year-old brother Radu were sent to Anatolia as hostages. They stayed there for six years. Radu was a handsome boy who caught the eye of the future sultan and life for him in the Turk court was luxurious. Vlad, on the other hand, was not so attractive and the conditions in captivity were consequently harsher.

In 1448 their father was assassinated and their elder brother was burnt alive by a rival claimant to the throne who was backed by the Hungarians. The Turks did not want a Hungarian vassal in control of Wallachia, so they released Vlad who returned home, while Radu stayed on in Turkey. With the help of the Turks, Vlad seized the throne, but after two months he was forced to flee into exile in Moldavia. The new ruler of Wallachia then struck a deal with Turkey, so Vlad sought Hungarian backing and, eight years later, returned to Wallachia and seized the throne once more.

The following six years of his rule were characterized by needless cruelty. Five hundred Wallachian boyars who had opposed his rule were rounded up. The older ones were impaled; the younger ones worked to death building Vlad's mountain fortress at Poenari.

According to one widely disseminated tale, two Italian ambassadors once arrived at his court. When they came to him they bowed and removed their hats, but kept on the berets they wore beneath them. When asked why they did not take off their caps, the ambassadors replied that it was their custom, and they did not even remove them for the Emperor. Vlad offered to 'reinforce' their custom for them, and ordered his servants to nail the unfortunate men's berets to their heads. In some versions of the story the diplomats were Turkish and the berets turbans, but the essence is the same.

According to another story: 'Dracula was very concerned that all his subjects work and contribute to the common welfare. He once noticed that the poor, vagrants, beggars and cripples had become very numerous in his land. Consequently, he issued an invitation to all the poor and sick in Wallachia to come to Târgoviste for a great feast, claiming that no one should go hungry in his land. As the poor and crippled arrived in the city they were ushered into a great hall where a fabulous feast was prepared for them. The prince's guests ate and drank late into the night, when Dracula himself made an appearance. 'What else do you desire? Do you want to be without cares, lacking nothing in this world?' asked the prince. When they responded in the affirmative, Dracula ordered the hall boarded up and set on fire. None escaped the flames. Dracula explained his action to the boyars by claiming that he did this 'in order that they represent no further burden to others and so that no one will be poor in my realm.'

When in 1459 the merchants of Brasov refused to pay their taxes despite repeated warnings, Dracula led an assault on the town, burning an entire suburb, and impaling numerous captives on Timpa Hill. The scene was immortalized in an especially gruesome woodcut which appeared as the frontispiece in a pamphlet printed in Nuremberg in 1499. It shows Vlad eating a meal while his men hack off limbs of victims beside the table. According to the narrative: 'Here begins a very cruel frightening story about a wild bloodthirsty man, Prince Dracula. How he impaled people and roasted them and boiled their heads in a kettle and skinned people and hacked them to pieces like cabbage. He roasted children and forced their mothers to eat them. And many other horrible things are written in this tract and in the land he ruled'.

When Vlad fell out with the Hungarian king, he began torturing and killing Transylvanian merchants, impaling them and their families on wooden stakes. According to one account: 'In the year 1460, on the morning of St Bartholomew's Day, Dracula ... had all the Hungarians of both sexes tracked down outside the village of Humilasch, and he was able to bring so many together that he piled them up in a bunch and he cut them up like cabbage with swords, sabres and knives; as for their chaplain and the others whom he did not kill there, he led them back home and had them impaled. And he had the village completely burned up with their goods and it is said that there were more than thirty thousand men'.

Although impalement had been practised by the French, the Spanish, and the Turks, it would become synonymous with Vlad, who turned it into a gruesome artform, often arranging the stakes on which he impaled his victims in complex designs. He made sure the stakes were not so sharp that the victim would die quickly of shock, and some reports have him oiling the stakes to ease their ingress. Some survived for hours, if not days. He used impalement to punish even quite minor crimes in his drive for law and order. He killed merchants who cheated their customers. He killed women who had affairs. It is said that he even had one woman impaled because her husband's shirt was too short. Even children were not safe from impalement. Dracula also had people skinned or boiled alive, and would afterwards display the corpses in public so everyone would learn a lesson. It is estimated that he killed anywhere between 40,000 and 100,000 people and it was said that over 20,000 corpses were displayed outside his capital city Târgoviste. His stern policy on law and order worked: to prove it, he had a gold cup placed on the drinking fountain in the main square of the capital. No one stole it.

It was the Turks, his principal enemy of the time, who named him 'the impaling prince'. There is no record of him using the epithet himself and in Romania he is known as Vlad Tepes. Having fallen out with the Hungarians, Vlad had to turn once more to the Turks for support, but when Vlad refused to pay a tribute of 10,000 ducats and 500 youths, the Ottoman Sultan Muhammad II the Conqueror rode into Wallachia. Falling back in front of the invading army, Vlad burned villages, poisoned wells and drove victims of infectious diseases into the Turkish camp. When the Turks finally reached Târgoviste, they were unprepared for the sight that greeted them.

'The Sultan's army came across a field with stakes, about three kilometres long and one kilometre wide,' wrote the Greek historian Chalcondyles.

*Portrait of Vlad
Tepes from a
painting in Castle
Ambras in the Tyrol.*

'And there were large stakes on which they could see the impaled bodies of men, women, and children, about twenty thousand of them… The Sultan, in wonder, kept saying that he could not conquer the country of a man who could do such terrible and unnatural things, and put his power and his subjects to such use. He also used to say that this man who did such things would be capable of worse. The other Turks were scared out of their wits. There were babies clinging to their mothers on the stakes, and birds had made nests in their breasts.'

Muhammad was so frightened he withdrew. Instead he sent Radu who, with defecting boyars and Turkish troops, drove Vlad back to his mountain fortress at Poenari. Vlad escaped across the Carpathians into Transylvania, but was arrested near Brasov by the Hungarian king Matthis Corvinus. Forged letters were circulated which indicated that it was Vlad who was a traitor to the Christian cause, not Radu.

Vlad ingratiated himself to his captors by converting from Orthodox Christianity to Catholicism. He was held under house arrest, though it is said that he kept his hand in by impaling rats and birds. When Radu died of syphilis in 1475, the throne of Wallachia fell into the hands of the rival Danesti clan. In 1476, with the backing of the Hungarians, Vlad returned to Wallachia again and reclaimed the throne. But that winter, the Turks invaded and Vlad was killed in battle. The circumstances of his death remain unclear. He might have been killed by his own side, who mistook him for a Turk, or he may have been assassinated by Basarab Laiota, who was to succeed him. Either way his severed head was taken by the Turks to Constantinople where it was stuck on a pole high above the city. It is thought that his body was taken by monks of the Snagov Monastery, whose renovation he had paid for some years earlier. They were said to have buried his body near the high altar, but an excavation in the 1930s failed to find it.

Stories of his cruelty circulated in German as early as 1463. Soon they spread throughout Europe, aided by the recent invention of the printing press. At least thirteen pamphlets detailing his crimes appeared between 1488 and 1521. Russian versions of the story praise his dedication to firm government, the Turks dwell on his atrocities, while to the Wallachians he is a hero who repeatedly repelled the Turkish invaders.

According to a German pamphlet published in Nuremberg in 1488: 'He had some of his people buried naked up to the navel and had them shot at. He also had some roasted and flayed. He captured the young Dan [of the rival Danesti clan] and had a grave dug for him and held a Christian funeral service and beheaded him beside the grave.

'He had a large pot made and boards with holes fastened over it and had people's heads shoved through there and imprisoned them in this. And he had the pot filled with water and a big fire made under it and let the people cry out pitiably until they were boiled to death.

'He devised dreadful, frightful, unspeakable torments, such as impaling together mothers and children nursing at their breasts so that the children kicked convulsively at their mothers' breasts until dead. In like manner he cut open mothers' breasts and stuffed their children's heads through and thus impaled both.

'He had all kinds of people impaled sideways: Christians, Jews, heathens, so that they moved and twitched and whimpered in confusion a long time like frogs... about three hundred gypsies came into his country.

Then he selected the best three of them and had them roasted; these the others had to eat.'

Although the truth of these stories is difficult to verify, they sometimes appear three or more times separately in seemingly independent accounts, lending them at least an appearance of credibility.

## Life and Crimes

| | |
|---|---|
| **c.1431** | Born Sighisoara in Transylvania. |
| **1436** | Moves to Wallachian capital Târgoviste when his father Vlad Dracul becomes prince. |
| **1442** | Sent as hostage to the court of the Ottoman sultan. |
| **1448** | Returns to Wallachia; names himself prince, but is forced to flee. |
| **1456–1462** | Institutes reign of terror on his return to Wallachia; thousands slaughtered. |
| **1462** | Turkish invasion forces him to flee to Hungary. |
| **1476** | Becomes ruler of Wallachia again, briefly, before being killed in December. |

# Richard III
## ◄ 1452–1485 ►
## KING OF ENGLAND

The youngest son of the Duke of York, Richard made his bloodthirsty way to the throne during the Wars of the Roses.

His older brother Edward IV had been deposed by Henry VI. Richard commanded the Yorkist forces at Barnet and Tewkesbury which put Edward back on the throne again, and there is evidence to suggest that Richard had a hand in the murder of the deposed Henry VI. He also commanded in the invasion of France in 1475 and disapproved of the peace treaty signed with Louis XI.

He went on to take control of the north of England, arranging raids into Scotland, resulting in all-out war in 1480. Two years later, Richard recaptured Berwick-on-Tweed, the last time the Royal Burgh of Berwick changed hands.

When Edward IV died, the crown passed to his 12-year-old son Edward V, with Richard as his 'protector'. He was opposed by Edward's mother and her family, the Woodvilles.

Richard had members of the Woodville family executed for treason. The dowager queen and other surviving Woodvilles sought sanctuary in

*Richard III: is his reputation justified, or does it simply verify the adage 'history is written by the victors'?*

Westminster Abbey. They were accused of plotting to murder him. Baron Hastings, an ardent Yorkist, was accused of conspiring with them and summarily executed.

Joining forces with the Duke of Buckingham, Richard had others arrested and executed until the queen gave up Edward's nine-year-old brother to join Edward in the Tower where kings customarily awaited their coronation.

Preachers in London then declared Edward IV's marriage illegal. That made Edward V and his brother illegitimate, leaving Richard as heir. On 26 June 1483, he became king. The two young princes disappeared in August – murdered, it seems, by Richard.

Buckingham rebelled raising a substantial force from his estates in Wales and the Marches, but his rebellion was failed when a storm prevented the landing of reinforcements from France and he was executed. However, this left Richard's forces weakened.

In August 1485, Henry Tudor landed in Wales. At the battle of Bosworth Field Richard was defeated and killed, and the Wars of the Roses were over. Thanks to William Shakespeare, Richard went on to become one of the greatest villains in English literature.

## Life and Crimes

**1452**  Born 2 October at Fotheringhay Castle, Northamptonshire.

**1460**  Older brother Edward IV takes the throne.

**1461**  Made Duke of Gloucester.

**1470**  Forced into exile with Edward IV.

**1471**  Returns to depose Henry VI and, in likelihood, murder him.

**1483**  Richard becomes 'protector' of Edward V; Richard seizes the throne; princes disappear in the Tower.

**1485**  Dies 22 August, Bosworth, Leicestershire.

# Cesare Borgia
### ◄ 1475–1507 ►
## CARDINAL OF ROME

Son of Pope Alexander VI, Cesare Borgia was a Renaissance captain who used the armies of the Church in an attempt to establish his own principality in central Italy. His manipulation of political power for his own ends is celebrated in *The Prince* by Niccolo Machiavelli.

Born to an old Spanish family in September 1475, Cesare was the son of Cardinal Rodrigo Borgia, who would become Pope Alexander VI, and his most famous mistress Vannozza Catanei. Famously debauched, Rodrigo had three children by earlier mistresses and four by Vannozza, one of whom, Lucrezia, became mistress to both her father and brother. Rodrigo also used murder as a political tool. No one was safe.

At the age of 16, Cesare became bishop of Pamplona. By 18, he was a cardinal and one of his father's closest advisers. But with his taste for prostitutes and incest, Cesare was not suited to the religious life. He therefore arranged the murder of his brother Juan, commander of the papal armies, and took over his job. He resigned as cardinal in 1498 and made a politically advantageous marriage to the sister of the King of Navarre, even though, by this time, his face was so ravaged by syphilis he had to wear a mask.

With the help of his French allies, he began to expand the Papal States and carve out a Borgia enclave. He forced Lucrezia into marriage for his own political advantage, murdering one of her husbands when it became convenient to do so. He also carried out a number of political murders himself, mainly of members of the rival Orsini family. His huge army terrorized the inhabitants of the region he occupied and he used rape as a political weapon. Machiavelli praised him as he believed that Cesare's ambition was to reunite Italy. Cesare himself took the motto: 'Aut Caesar aut nihil' – 'Either Caesar or nothing'.

When Pope Alexander VI died suddenly in 1503, Cesare was arrested by Alexander's successor, Julius II, a bitter foe of the Borgias. Forced to surrender the cities he had taken, Cesare fled to Naples, which was then under the control of Spain. But the Spanish refused to join him in a war on the pope and imprisoned him. He escaped to Navarre, where he was killed in an ambush at the age of 31.

## Life and Crimes

**1475** Born in September in Rome.

**1491** Becomes bishop of Pamplona.

**1493** Becomes cardinal and the pope's principal adviser.

**1497** Arranges murder of his brother and takes command of the papal armies.

**1498** Resigns as cardinal and marries to make an alliance with France.

**1499** Occupies cities of the Romagna and Marches; takes Imola and Forlí.

**1500** Murders brother-in-law.

**1501** Takes Rimini, Pesaro and Faenza.

**1502** Captures Urbino, Camerino and Senigallia, executing those who opposed him there.

**1503** Father, Pope Alexander VI, dies 18 August; Cesare arrested.

**1506** Escapes from prison in Spain.

**1507** Killed in action outside Viana in Navarre 12 March.

# Francisco Pizarro

◄ c. 1475–1541 ►

## CONQUEROR OF THE INCAS

The illegitimate son of an army officer, Francisco Pizarro was abandoned by his parents. He had no schooling, could neither read nor write and earned a living as a swineherd before he became a soldier.

In 1502, he sailed to Hispaniola to seek his fortune, then in 1510 joined an expedition to Colombia. On a second expedition with Nuñez de Balboa in 1513, he crossed the Isthmus of Panama and caught his first glimpse of the Pacific. When Balboa was beheaded by Pedrarias Dávila, Pizarro switched his allegiance to Dávila and was sent to trade with the natives down the Pacific coast. He helped Dávila subdue the warlike tribes in Panama and in 1520 undertook an expedition to Costa Rica.

In 1522, news of Hernán Cortés's slaughter of the Aztecs and the resulting haul of gold fired Pizarro with enthusiasm. With Diego de Almagro, another soldier of fortune, he set sail to begin a series of expeditions along the coast of South America. Conditions were appalling and many of his men died, but in 1528 he returned to Panama from Peru laden with gold. When the governor of Panama refused him permission to make further expeditions, Pizarro took his case to the king back in Spain. In return for delivering Peru to the crown, he was named a knight of Santiago and viceroy of whatever lands he might conquer.

In June 1530, Pizarro sailed for the empire of the Incas with four of his brothers, 180 men and thirty-seven horses. After early difficulties, they succeeded in devastating a coastal settlement, despite the hospitality they had received from the locals. When reinforcements arrived, they invited the Inca ruler Atahuallpa to visit their camp. He turned up with a body guard, but they were unarmed. Pizarro then insisted that he accept Christianity and the sovereignty of the King of Spain. When Atahuallpa rejected both, throwing the Bible to the ground, Pizarro opened up with artillery on Atahuallpa's unarmed followers, massacring them.

The Inca army camped nearby was now leaderless and retreated into the interior. Atahuallpa himself was held for a ransom of enough gold and silver to fill the room he was being held in. When it was paid, Atahuallpa was strangled. Almagro then pushed on to take and devastate the Inca capital Cuzco, while Pizarro founded the Spanish capital Lima.

Pizarro had Manco Capac crowned king of the Incas in an attempt to control them. But Manco turned on his patron, and Lima was saved only by the arrival of some of Cortés's men.

Meanwhile Almagro had travelled on to Chile but, finding it poor, he returned to Peru where he rescued Pizarro's brothers from a siege in Cuzco, taking the town as his share of the spoils. Pizarro then sent troops from Lima, who defeated Almagro. He was imprisoned and executed. Pizarro spent the rest of his life trying to consolidate his power in Peru.

On 26 June 1541, Pizarro was assassinated by a group of Almagro supporters, led by Almagro's son. Pizarro himself had four children by native women, including a son by a relative of Atahuallpa who was never legitimized.

## Life and Crimes

**c.1475**  Born at Trujillo, Extremadura, Castile.
**1502**  Sails for Hispaniola.
**1510**  Joins expedition to Colombia.
**1513**  Sees Pacific.
**1522**  Enters partnership with Almagro.
**1528**  Returns from Peru with gold; appointed viceroy of all the lands he conquers.
**1530**  Sails from Panama.
**1532**  Takes Atahuallpa, emperor of the Incas, hostage.
**1533**  Strangles Atahuallpa.
**1535**  Founds city of Lima.
**1537**  Almagro takes Inca capital of Cuzco.
**1541**  Pizarro assassinated 26 June in Lima.

# Hernán Cortés
## ◄ 1485–1547 ►
## DESTROYER OF THE AZTECS

The young Spanish nobleman Hernán Cortés destroyed the Aztec empire, turning against his Spanish masters to become ruler of New Spain, now known as Mexico.

Cortés conquered the Aztec empire with just 500 men, 16 horses and a few cannons. Almost as important was his mistress, a slave girl called Malinche, later baptized as Doña Marina. She spoke both Mayan and the Aztec language Natuatl and acted crucially as his interpreter throughout the campaign.

The Aztecs had an inkling of their fate when, between 1507 and 1510, strange ships began to be seen off the coast of Mexico. Then came a series of ill omens – a comet appeared in the sky, lightning struck a temple and the sound of women weeping was heard at night. Although the Aztec ruler Motecuhzoma simply executed anyone who reported these portents of doom, it did no good. According to Aztec legends, the god Quetzalcoatl, the mythical ruler of the Toltecs, the Aztecs' precursors, had been exiled and would return in the year I Reed, according to the Aztec calendar. I Reed was 1519, the very year Cortés arrived from Cuba.

Naturally Motecuhzoma assumed that they were gods and that their ships were wooden temples. He sent gold and magnificent costumes made out of feathers, in the hope that the gods would take the gifts and go. Instead Cortés seized the messengers and put them in chains. He gave them a demonstration of his god-like powers by firing his cannons, which made the Aztecs faint. Cortés established himself at Veracruz and burnt his ships so that his men could not flee, then began his march on the Aztec capital Tenochtitlán.

With armour, muskets, crossbows, swords and horses, the Spanish had overwhelming military superiority. War for peoples of pre-Columbian Mexico was largely a ceremonial affair. They wore elaborate costumes and were armed only with a small sword made out of obsidian – volcanic glass. Their object was to capture as many of the enemy as possible to use as human sacrifices later. If a leader was killed or a temple captured, the loser capitulated immediately and talks began over the amount of tribute that should be paid. Cortés simply did not play by the rules. He slaughtered as many as he could on the battlefield.

Motecuhzoma's only possible defence was guile. He tried to capture Cortés in an ambush at Cholula. But Cortés discovered the plan and massacred the citizens of Cholula. He destroyed the temple of Huitzilopochtli, the Aztec god of war, there and set up an image of the Virgin Mary instead. It was a key psychological victory.

Cortés established an alliance with the people of Tlaxcala, who had only recently been conquered by Motecuhzoma. They rebelled and more subject peoples rallied to Cortés. Hearing what had happened at Cholula, other Aztec cities surrendered without a fight and Cortés marched on Tenochtitlán unopposed.

Motecuhzoma had no choice but to greet the Spanish graciously. He lodged Cortés in the palace of Axayacatl, Motecuhzoma's father, which was packed with gold ornaments. The Spanish melted these down, throwing away the decorative stones and feathers. The gold was shipped as bars and sent directly to Charles V in Spain, bypassing Cortés's commander, the governor of Cuba, Diego Velázquez. Cortés also demanded that Motecuhzoma swear allegiance to Charles V of Spain. He was to remain nominal ruler of the Aztecs while Cortés himself seized the reins of power, with the aim of becoming viceroy.

To reassert his authority, Velázquez sent a force of over 1,000 under Panfilo de Narváez to bring Cortés to heel. Leaving a small force under Pedro de Alvardo in Tenochtitlán, Cortés headed back to the coast where he defeated Narváez and used his troops to swell his own ranks.

Meanwhile, in Tenochtitlán, the Aztecs were celebrating the festival of their war god Huitzilopochtli which, like all Aztec festivals, involved human sacrifice on an epic scale. Terrified by the extent of these bloodthirsty rituals, Alvardo's men turned on the Aztecs and slaughtered as many as 10,000 priests and worshippers. When Cortés returned to Tenochtitlán, he found the city in a state of open warfare. He tried to calm the situation by getting Motecuhzoma to talk to his people, but the Aztecs stoned Motecuhzoma to death as a traitor.

Cortés grabbed as much gold and treasure and his men could carry and tried to make a run for it. The Aztecs ambushed them and Cortés escaped with just 500 men. But in a monumental tactical error, the Aztecs did not pursue the Spanish and finish them off. This allowed Cortés to regroup. He turned back and laid siege to the city.

The Aztecs put up fierce resistance. But for months, they were starved and harried. Finally they were defeated by an epidemic of smallpox brought by one of Narváez's soldiers. This killed Motecuhzoma's successor, his brother Cuitlahuac. Their cousin Cuahtemoc took over as emperor, but he was captured and tortured until he revealed fresh sources of gold. Later he was hanged on the pretext of treason against Charles V.

Many of the priests and Aztec soldiers preferred to die rather than surrender to the Spanish. To quell any resistance, Cortés demolished Tenochtitlán, building by building, using the rubble to fill in the city's waterways that had served as streets in the manner of Venice. Mexico City was built on the ruins. The surviving Aztecs were used as slave labour in the gold and silver mines. They were decimated by two further epidemics of smallpox. Forcible conversion to Christianity destroyed what remained of their culture and they lost themselves in drink.

What little we know of the Aztecs comes from Cortés and his men, who were more interested in booty than scholarship, and the Franciscan friar Bernardino de Sahagún who circulated questionnaires among survivors of the onslaught in an attempt to learn something of the culture they had destroyed. His work was inhibited by the Inquisition who investigated him for being too pro-Indian and confiscated his writings which, fortunately, resurfaced in the eighteenth century.

Cortés led an expedition to Honduras in 1524. Returning to Spain to plead his case in 1528 he was confirmed a captain general. Back in 1530, he put down civil unrest and retired to his estates at Cuernavaca, 30 miles south of Mexico City, where he built a palace. In 1536, he led an expedition to Baja California, but when a viceroy was appointed he returned to Spain. Eventually he was given permission to return to New Spain, but died in Seville in 1547 before he could make the journey.

# Life and Crimes

**1485**  Born at Medellín, Castile.

**1489**  Attends University of Salamanca where he is 'much given to women'.

**1504**  Sails for the island of Hispaniola, now Santo Domingo.

**1509**  Misses ill-fated expedition to mainland of South America after contracting syphilis.

**1519**  Lands in Mexico.

**1520**  After witnessing bloodthirsty Aztec rituals, his men slaughter 10,000.

**1521**  Besieges then razes the Aztec capital Tenochtitlán.

**1524**  Leads expedition to Honduras.

**1528**  Returns to Spain and is confirmed as captain general.

**1530**  Puts down civil unrest in New Spain.

**1536**  Leads expedition to Baja California.

**1540**  Returns to Spain once more.

**1547**  Dies 2 December in Seville.

# Henry VIII
## ◀ 1491–1547 ▶
## KING OF ENGLAND

When Henry VIII came to the throne, he seemed to be the ideal king – young, fit, well educated and handsome. He was to become a bloody tyrant.

Fond of hunting and playing tennis, he also wrote music and books – including an attack on Martin Luther which earned him the title 'Defender of the Faith', conferred on him by the pope. In 1502, his older brother Arthur died and he became heir to the throne. In 1509, Henry succeeded his father Henry VII, who had given England twenty-four years of peace after putting an end to the Wars of the Roses. Henry VIII saw that his first duty as king was to produce an heir to spare England from any further wars of succession.

It was also vital to England's interests that she maintain an alliance with Spain, so Henry married Arthur's widow, Catherine of Aragon, on the understanding that her former marriage had not been consummated. Although it was a marriage of political convenience, it also seems to have been a love match – at first, at least.

His father had left the royal household's finances in good order, so Henry VIII had no reason to call a parliament to raise taxes. He left the running of the government to his Lord Chancellor Thomas Wolsey, who exercised his powers through the court of Chancery and the infamous court of the Star Chamber. In 1515, Wolsey was made a cardinal and papal legate to England, and he built Hampton Court Palace – which was far grander than anything the king possessed.

Henry concentrated his energies on foreign policy. A Scottish invasion was repelled at the Battle of Flodden in 1513 and he pursued several campaigns against France, concluding a peace at the Field of the Cloth of Gold in 1520. He also built up the Royal Navy, recalling Parliament in 1523 to pay for it. The following year, he imposed a special levy which met such fierce opposition he was forced to rescind it, leaving both Henry and Wolsey both deeply unpopular and Henry practically bankrupt.

While Catherine had given birth to a live baby girl, Princess Mary, in 1516, she failed to give Henry the male heir he craved. Catherine was now in her forties and Henry had fallen in love with Anne Boleyn, the sister of a mistress who had borne him an illegitimate son. He appealed to the pope to grant him a divorce from Catherine on the grounds that a man was not allowed to marry his brother's widow, even though the pope had given Henry a special dispensation to do so.

Normally there would have been no problem, but at that time Pope Clement VII was under the control of the Holy Roman Emperor Charles V, Catherine's nephew. Unable to get a divorce, Henry went ahead and married Anne Boleyn without the pope's permission and broke with the Church of Rome, declaring himself to be supreme head of the church in England. He closed down the English monasteries and seized their wealth, and killed all those who opposed him – including his own Lord Chancellor Sir Thomas More, who was executed for treason for refusing to acknowledge Henry as head of the Church of England. His chief minister Cardinal Wolsey fell into disfavour for failing to secure the divorce. He died before he could be executed and Henry took over his palace at Hampton Court.

Wolsey was replaced by Thomas Cromwell, who introduced legislation turning England towards Protestantism. Increasing government control caused a rebellion called the Pilgrimage of Grace in 1536. A 30,000-strong rebel army was raised in the north. However, vague promises and assurances persuaded them to disband. Sporadic riots the following year allowed Henry's administration to pick off the opposition piecemeal. In all some 220 to 250 rebels were executed.

When Anne also failed to produce a male heir, he accused her of adultery. She was sentenced to be burnt alive, but Henry mercifully commuted the sentence to beheading and brought in a skilled swordsman from Calais to do the job. He was not so merciful to the five young men, including Anne's brother, who were accused of being her lovers: after being tortured into confessing, they were hanged, drawn and quartered.

Henry now married Jane Seymour who gave him a son, but he was a weakly child and she died shortly after. Henry married again, to a foreign princess, Anne of Cleves, in a match engineered by Thomas Cromwell in order to secure a Lutheran alliance in northern Europe, but found she was not to his taste, describing her dismissively as the 'Flanders mare'. Cromwell was arrested and executed, leaving Henry to force through legislation giving more power to the throne.

Henry's fifth wife, the 19-year-old Catherine Howard, was executed for adultery when it was discovered that she was not a virgin when she had married him. Francis Dereham, who had taken her virginity was hanged, drawn and quartered, while Thomas Culpepper, who was found guilty of sleeping with Catherine after the marriage, only suffered the comparatively merciful punishment of beheading as he was one of Henry's favourites.

Henry married once again, for the sixth time, to Katherine Parr, who was to outlive him.

Although England remained a strong country after Henry, the legacy of the political and religious differences he engendered remains to this day.

## Life and Crimes

**1491**  Born 28 June in Greenwich.
**1509**  Succeeds to the throne on 22 April.
**1527**  Sends Cardinal Wolsey to seek divorce from Rome on his behalf.
**1529**  Ousts Wolsey after no divorce is forthcoming.
**1533**  Marries Anne Boleyn; breaks with Rome and becomes head of the Church of England.
**1536**  Executes Anne.
**1536–40**  Dissolves monasteries.
**1542**  Executes Catherine Howard.
**1547**  Dies 28 January in London.

# Mary I
### ◀ 1516–1558 ▶
## QUEEN OF ENGLAND

Mary Tudor was the first queen to rule England in her own right. Her brutal persecution of Protestants earned her the nickname 'Bloody Mary'.

The daughter of Henry VIII and Catherine of Aragon, she found herself declared illegitimate when Henry dissolved his marriage in 1533. She was stripped of her title of princess and forced to renounce her Catholic faith, though she continued to practise it secretly.

On the death of her half-brother, the weakly Edward VI, a Protestant insurrection put Lady Jane Grey on the throne and Mary fled to Norfolk. The general feeling in the country though, was that Mary was the rightful heir, and she returned to a triumphal welcome in London. Lady Jane Grey – the so-called 'Nine Days Queen' – was deposed after just two weeks on the throne and executed, along with her husband Dudley.

*Mary I had no sympathy for those who refused to convert to Catholicism and burned hundreds of Protestants at the stake.*

Soon after her coronation Mary began to revive the Catholic Church which had been banned under Henry VIII. When it became clear that she was going to marry the Catholic Philip, king of Spain, there was a Protestant rising in Kent under Sir Thomas Wyatt, leading to a march on London by the Kentishmen. Mary gave a rousing speech which stirred the people of the capital to defend her, and the rebellion was defeated and its leaders executed.

Mary then married Philip, restored the Catholic creed and began persecuting heretics. Some 300 Protestants were burnt at the stake. Her marriage to Philip embroiled England in an unpopular war with France, which lost her Calais, England's last toehold in France.

Lonely, childless and hated, she died on 17 November 1558, to be succeeded by her half-sister Elizabeth I, a Protestant.

## Life and Crimes

**1516**  Born 18 February in Greenwich.

**1533**  Declared illegitimate and stripped of her title.

**1534**  Forced to abandon Catholic faith.

**1544**  Allowed to return to court and re-admitted to the succession.

**1553**  Ascends to the throne.

**1554**  Puts down Wyatt rebellion, executing leaders; marries Philip II of Spain.

**1555–1558**  Burns some 300 Protestants at the stake.

**1558**  Loses Calais; dies childless on 17 November in London.

# Catherine de'Medici
◄ 1519–1589 ►
## REGENT OF FRANCE

Catherine de'Medici came from the powerful Medici family which ruled Florence with despotic powers almost continuously from 1434 to 1737. In 1533, she married the second son of Francis I, Henry, Duke of Orléans, who became Henry II in 1547. Although he maintained a very public mistress, Diane of Poitiers, Catherine bore him ten children in ten years of marriage. Nevertheless, as queen, she had very little influence while Diane took her place at the centre of power, dispensing patronage and accepting favours.

Henry II died in 1559 when he was accidentally hit on the head with a lance by one of his Scots Guards and was succeeded by 15-year-old Francis II who was married to Mary Queen of Scots. Catherine quickly assumed control. She excluded Diane from the deathbed and Henry's funeral. Diane was forced to return the crown jewels and evicted from the Château de Chenonceau which Henry had given her.

At the time, France was split by a series of religious wars between the Catholics, who were backed by Spain, and the Protestants, led by a group called the Huguenots. Initially they were not considered a threat, but when the Protestant Prince of Condé began raising an army in the south she ordered him to attend court and had him arrested.

He was convicted of treason and sentenced to death. But realizing that Francis was ill and likely to die she got Condé's brother Antoine de Bourbon, First Prince of the Blood, to renounce his right to the regency in exchange for his life. So when Francis died in 1560 and her ten-year-old son Charles took the throne, Catherine became regent.

In that role, she attempted to make peace between the Catholics and the Protestants. Nevertheless, unrest, bloodshed and civil war – punctuated with the occasional peace treaty ensued.

Catherine attempted to end the conflict in 1572 by ordering the massacre of over 4,000 Huguenots in Paris, in what became known as the St Bartholomew's Day Massacre. Pope Gregory XIII struck a medal to celebrate the event. But instead of ending the conflict, it provoked a renewal of hostilities.

She became regent again when Charles IX died in 1574 and, during the reign of Henry III, continued dabbling in politics, stoking up religious conflict.

# Life and Crimes

**1519**  Born 13 April in Florence.

**1533**  Marries Henry, Duke of Orléans.

**1547**  Becomes queen consort.

**1559**  Husband Henry II dies.

**1560**  Son Francis II dies; Catherine becomes regent.

**1572**  Orders the murder of the Huguenots in the St Bartholomew's Day Massacre.

**1574**  Becomes regent once more.

**1589**  Dies 5 January at Blois in France.

# Ivan the Terrible

## ◄ 1530–1584 ►

## TSAR OF RUSSIA

Coming to the Muscovite throne at the age of three when his father died, Ivan lived in fear of the warrior caste of 'boyars' and witnessed the terrible acts of torture and cruelty they performed in his name.

When his uncle Yuri challenged his right to the throne, he was arrested and thrown in a dungeon, where he was left to starve. Ivan's mother, who was otherwise indifferent to the child, assumed power as regent and had another of Ivan's uncles killed. A short time afterwards she died suddenly, probably poisoned. Ivan was just eight years old. A week later his mother's consort, Prince Ivan Obolensky, was arrested and beaten to death by his jailers, and Obolensky's sister Agrafena, Ivan's beloved nurse, was sent to a convent.

Without Agrafena, there was no one to whom Ivan could turn for help or advice. The boyars alternately neglected and molested him and his brother Yuri, a deaf-mute, leaving them to go about hungry and in rags. Ivan was a beggar in his own palace. When a rivalry between two boyar families, the Shuiskys and the Belskys, escalated into a bloody feud, armed men roamed the palace, seeking out their enemies and frequently bursting into Ivan's quarters, where they smashed the place up and took whatever they wanted. Verbal and physical abuse, beatings and murders became commonplace. Ivan was an intelligent and sensitive boy and an insatiable reader. Unable to strike back, he took out his frustrations on defenceless animals, tearing the feathers off birds, piercing their eyes and slitting open their bodies.

In 1539 the Shuiskys led a raid on the palace, rounding up a number of Ivan's remaining confidants. The loyal Fyodor Mishurin was skinned alive and left on public display in a Moscow square. But on 29 December 1543, the 13-year-old Ivan suddenly struck back. He ordered the arrest of the sadistic Prince Andrew Shuisky and had him thrown into a pen with a pack of starved hunting dogs.

Although boyar rule had ended, the people of Moscow found themselves little better off. By the time he took power, Ivan was already a disturbed young man and a heavy drinker. He threw dogs and cats from the Kremlin walls, enjoying watching them suffer as they hit the ground below. He roamed the Moscow streets with a street gang, drinking, mugging old people and raping women, disposing of his victims by having them strangled, hanged, buried alive or thrown to the bears.

An excellent horseman, he was fond of hunting: besides the thrill of the kill, Ivan also enjoyed beating up and robbing farmers. On the other hand, Ivan was often very devout. He would prostrate himself before icons and bang his head against the floor until his forehead was callused. He even made a public confession of his sins in Moscow, and in his quieter moments, devoted himself to books, mainly religious and historical texts.

At the age of 17, he was crowned Tsar of Russia. Soon after, a mysterious fire destroyed much of Moscow. Ivan blamed the Glinskys – a prominent family of boyars to which his mother belonged – and turned the mob against them. He then set about building an empire.

He centralized government, but ruled with the help of a 'selected council'. He quickly expanded his territory to the east of the Urals, but was defeated by the Crimean Tartars and the Lithuanians. He reduced corruption and the remaining influence of the boyar families, and reformed the Church and the army, creating an elite force, the *Streltsy*. And in 1558 he started trading directly with England.

It was necessary for him to marry and the noble families of Russia all pushed their daughters forward. He chose Anastasia – a Romanov – who had a stabilizing effect on him. But when she died in 1560, after bearing him six children, he became mentally unstable again. He smashed up the furniture and banged his head on the floor in front of the court. Angry and depressed, he became increasingly paranoid. He became convinced that the boyars had poisoned Anastasia. Although he had no evidence against them, he had a number of boyars tortured and executed. He dissolved the selected council and took power into his own hands, unleashing a reign of terror. Thousands were tortured and killed, and even his closest advisers were imprisoned or exiled. Lists that survive include some 4,000 names – though Ivan donated money to the church to pray for the souls of his victims...

However, when in 1564 he announced he was going to abdicate, people begged him to stay on, regarding rule by a mad tsar as preferable to another dose of boyar rule. Ivan agreed to remain Tsar on condition that he be paid a huge fee and given absolute power.

To enforce his rule Ivan introduced the 'Oprichniki', a hand-picked bunch of thugs who had to swear a personal oath of allegiance to Ivan. Dressed in black and riding black horses, they carried a severed dog's head on a pole as their emblem. The mere sight of the Oprichniki instilled fear in the populace. They could kill anyone of whom Ivan disapproved, and would not hesitate to burst into a church during mass and abduct the priest or murder him before the altar.

Ivan fortified his residence and ran it along the lines of a monastery – though Christian liturgy alternated with the sadistic torture of his enemies. The Oprichniki were formed into a pseudo-monastic order with Ivan as their abbot. They performed sacrilegious masses, followed by drunken orgies of rape and torture. Ivan would act as master of ceremonies, using red-hot pincers to tear the ribs out of men's chests. Afterwards he would throw himself down before the altar and repent, then rise and read sermons on the Christian virtues to his sated followers.

He carried an iron-tipped staff, with which he lashed out at anyone who offended him. Once, he had peasant women stripped naked and used for target practice, and on another occasion, he had several hundred beggars drowned in a lake. A boyar was forced to sit on a barrel of gunpowder and blown to bits. According to one biographer, Prince Boris Telupa 'was drawn upon a long sharp-made stake, which entered the lower part of his body and came out of his neck; upon which he languished in horrible pain for fifteen hours alive, and spoke to his mother, brought to behold that woeful sight. And she was given to 100 gunners, who defiled her to death, and the Emperor's hungry hounds devoured her flesh and bones'. Friends were no safer. His treasurer, Nikita Funikov, was boiled to death in a cauldron and his councillor, Ivan Viskovaty, was hanged, while Ivan's men took turns to hack pieces off his body.

In 1570, Ivan sacked and burned the city of Novgorod and tortured, mutilated, impaled, roasted and massacred 60,000 of its citizens. A German mercenary wrote: 'Mounting a horse and brandishing a spear, he charged in and ran people through while his son watched the entertainment....' The archbishop of Novgorod was sewn inside a bearskin and then hunted by a pack of hounds who tore him to pieces.

Men, women and children were tied to sleighs, which were pushed into the freezing waters of the Volkhov River. There were so many corpses they dammed the river and made it flood its banks. Novgorod never recovered. Later the city of Pskov suffered a similar fate.

After two years of bad harvests, Russia was hit by an epidemic of plague. Then in 1571, Moscow was devastated by a fire. Meanwhile the Swedes, Turks, Lithuanians and Crimean Tartars massed on Russia's borders. Narva was lost, but Ivan managed to repel the Tartar invasion after they had sacked Moscow. Then suddenly in 1572 Ivan dismissed the Oprichniki, reverted to the title of Prince of Moscow and installed a Tartar prince on the throne, only to have him exiled after a year.

His married life was just as eccentric. In 1561 he married a Circassian beauty, but he soon tired of her. Two years after her death in 1569 he married a merchant's daughter, but she died two weeks after the wedding. He suspected she had been poisoned and he had her brother impaled. In 1575, he got rid of his fourth wife by sending her to a convent. His fifth wife was soon replaced by a sixth. When she was discovered with a lover, he was impaled under her window, and wife number six joined wife number four in the convent. When Ivan discovered that his seventh wife was not a virgin, he had her drowned. His eighth wife seems to have outlived him. Meanwhile he boasted of deflowering a thousand virgins.

Despite his turbulent love life, Ivan maintained a good relationship with his eldest son, the young man he had entertained in Novgorod. But on 19 November 1581 Ivan had a row with his son's wife over the suitability of the clothes she was wearing. He beat her up, causing her to miscarry. Father and son then had a row. In a sudden fit of rage, Ivan the Terrible struck his son on the head with his metal-tipped staff. The Prince lay in a coma for several days before succumbing to a festering head wound. Ivan was overcome by grief, and allegedly never slept again, roaming his palace at night in an agony of remorse.

To the end of his life, Ivan was habitually bad-tempered and was seen to foam at the mouth like a horse. In his last years, he had to be carried on a litter. His body swelled, the skin peeled and gave off a terrible odour. As death neared, he took monastic vows.

Ivan fainted suddenly and died in 1584, as he was preparing to play a game of chess. Hardly a family in Russia had escaped his murderous rule unscathed and many had been eliminated completely. Farmers had fled their land in terror and countless acres had been reclaimed by the forests. The country would take centuries to recover from the activities of this most tyrannical of rulers.

## Life and Crimes

**1530** Born 25 August at Kolomenskoye near Moscow.

**1533** Succeeds father as Grand Prince of Moscow.

**1547** Becomes Tsar of Russia.

**1560** Begins reign of terror.

**1564** Threatens to abdicate; is persuaded to stay on as absolute monarch.

**1570** Orders massacre of 60,000 in Novgorod.

**1571** Defeated by Crimean Tartars who then raided Moscow.

**1581** Kills his own son.

**1584** Dies 18 March in Moscow.

# Toyotomi Hideyoshi
## ◄ 1536–1598 ►
### RULER OF JAPAN

Toyotomi Hideyoshi was the Supreme Daimyo of Japan from 1590 to 1598 and completed the unification of the country.

A foot soldier in the army of Oda Nobunga, who began the unification of Japan, Hideyoshi rose quickly through the ranks of the samurai, taking command when Nobunga committed suicide in 1582. Hideyoshi was also instrumental in creating the idea of the samurai as a 'warrior elite', a class apart who alone were allowed to carry weapons and wear armour. In warfare he was ruthless. Once he diverted a river through an enemy's castle, drowning everyone inside. He did not hesitate to take the heads of 1,000 enemy soldiers, and nor did he have any qualms about risking the lives of his own men.

When he took over the lands of other daimyos, he ordered them to destroy their fortifications and took their wives and children to Kyoto as hostages. For the offence of holding a single mercenary, he demanded the forfeit of three heads.

He drafted thousands of peasants for his enormous building projects, treating his workers harshly. He also levied punitive taxes, saying: 'Treat peasants like sesame seeds; the more you squeeze, the more you get.'

On one occasion some scribbling was detected on the gates of his palace. He had 20 suspects crucified. The notion of crucifixion seems to have amused him: in 1597, he had 26 Catholic priests crucified, who had come as missionaries to Japan.

Invading Korea in 1592 and 1597, he urged his men to cut off the noses and ears of the enemy as he planned to build a huge mound with them back home in Kyoto. Any officer who failed to carry out his orders or questioned them was summarily executed. It was during Hideyoshi's rule that the tea ceremony became popular amongst the warrior caste, and on this too, he had firm views: when the inoffensive master of the tea ceremony Sen no Rikyu offended against the strict code, he was first exiled, then ordered to commit suicide.

When Hideyoshi's only son died in 1591, he named his 23-year-old nephew Hidetsugu as his heir. When six months later a new son was unexpectedly born, Hidetsugu was no longer needed and in 1595 he was also sent into exile, then ordered to commit suicide. His young wife, their three children and his 30 concubines were paraded through the streets of Kyoto, then publicly executed. Their bodies were thrown into a pit over which a stone was erected, bearing the legend: 'Tomb of Traitors'.

## Life and Crimes

**1536**  Born in Nakamura, Owari province, Japan.
**1568**  Joins Oda Nobunga's campaign to subjugate central Japan.
**1582**  Succeeds to command when Nobunga commits suicide.
**1590**  Becomes Supreme Daimyo – military dictator – of a unified Japan.
**1592**  Attacks Korea.
**1595**  Orders death of his heir and executes his entire household.
**1597**  Invades Korea again.
**1598**  Dies 18 September at Fushimi.

# Elizabeth Bathory

◄ 1560–1614 ►

## COUNTESS OF TRANSYLVANIA

A legendary beauty, Elizabeth Bathory was born in 1560 into one of the oldest and wealthiest families in Transylvania. She had many powerful relatives, including a cardinal and several princes, a cousin who became prime minister of Hungary, and an uncle who became King Steven of Poland (1575–86). However, other relatives were known to be insane and sexually perverted, and another uncle was an infamous devil-worshipper.

At 15, Elizabeth married 26-year-old Count Ferencz Nasdasdy, but kept her surname. They moved into the mountain fortress Castle Csejthe, overlooking the village of Csejthe in the Nyitra country of north-west Hungary. The count spent so much time away from home fighting the Turks that he earned himself the nom de guerre 'The Black Hero of Hungary'. Left on her own, Elizabeth grew bored and took a series of young lovers. Her domineering mother-in-law came to stay. Elizabeth began to pay regular visits to her aunt, the Countess Klara Bathory, who was openly bisexual.

She also amused herself torturing servant girls: her favourite punishments included leaving them outside naked in the snow, or smearing their nude bodies with honey and leaving them where they would attract bees and insects.

Under the guidance of an old maid named Dorothea Szentes, who claimed to be a witch, she developed an interest in the occult. Dorothea Szentes, who was known as Dorka, also encouraged Elizabeth's sadistic tendencies and, together, they began disciplining the female servants in an underground torture chamber. With the aid of Dorka, Iloona Joo, Elizabeth's major-domo Johannes Ujvary and another witch named Anna Darvula, who was also allegedly Elizabeth's lesbian lover, Elizabeth indulged her perverted fantasies. She would find any excuses to punish young servant girls. The victim would be stripped naked, then whipped. Elizabeth liked to whip the girl's front rather than her back as it did more damage and she could watch her victim's face contort in pain. Another favourite was sticking pins in various sensitive places on the victim's body, such as under fingernails.

In 1600 Elizabeth's husband died. The first thing she did was banish her hated mother-in-law. Now there was no one to restrain her. One day a servant girl accidentally pulled her hair while combing it. Elizabeth slapped the girl so hard she drew blood. When the blood fell on her own hand she thought that her skin took on the freshness of that of her young maid. She was convinced that she found the secret of eternal youth. She had Johannes Ujvary and Dorka strip the maid, cut her arteries and drain her blood into a huge vat. Then Elizabeth bathed in it, convinced that it would beautify her entire body.

She continued the treatment for the next ten years, regularly bathing in the blood of girls hired as servants from Csejthe and the surrounding villages, then killed and mutilated. She also drank their blood to give her inner beauty. However, as time went on, she began to fear that the treatment was not quite the miracle cure she had been hoping for. She concluded that the blood of peasant girls was of inferior quality, so she sent out her henchmen to kidnap aristocratic girls, who met the same grisly fate. The disappearance of the daughters of the nobility did not go unnoticed.

In 1610 villagers saw the dead bodies of four girls being dumped over the ramparts; when one of the intended victims escaped and told the authorities about what was happening at Castle Csejthe, King Mathias II of Hungary ordered another of Elizabeth's cousins, Count Cuyorgy Thurzo, governor of the province, to investigate.

On the night of 30 December 1610, Thurzo raided Castle Csejthe with a band of soldiers. They were horrified by the terrible sights in the castle. One girl lay in the main room, her body drained of blood. Another, whose body had been pierced with holes, was still alive. In the dungeons they discovered several living girls, some of whom had been tortured. Below the castle, they exhumed the bodies of some fifty girls, and found a register of 650 victims in Elizabeth Bathory's bedroom.

But the Countess was of noble birth, so was not taken before a court and tried. She refused to plead and was kept under house arrest. Her four accomplices were tried in 1611 at Bitcse. Johannes Ujvary confessed to the murder of thirty-seven unmarried girls. The victims were tied up and cut with scissors. Sometimes the two witches, or the countess herself, tortured these girls before they were drained of blood, he said. Elizabeth's old nurse Iloona Joo confessed to the murder of some forty girls.

Dorothea Szentes and Anna Darvula were beheaded and cremated, while Johannes Ujvary and Iloona Joo had their fingers torn off and were burned alive. Although no court ever convicted Countess Elizabeth Bathory of any crime, she did not escape punishment. King Mathias wanted Elizabeth to face the death penalty for her crime, but out of respect for her cousin, his prime minister, he agreed to an indefinitely delayed sentence, essentially condemning her to solitary confinement for life. Stonemasons were brought to Castle Csejthe to brick up the windows and doors of the bedchamber with the countess inside. A small hole was left through which food could be passed. In 1614, four years after she had been walled in, a guard found her lying face down on the floor, dead at the age of 54.

## Life and Crimes

| | |
|---|---|
| **1560** | Born in Transylvania. |
| **1575** | Marries Count Ferencz Nasdasdy. |
| **1604–1610** | Tortures and killes female victims and bathes in their blood. |
| **1610** | Villagers spot bodies of dead girls being thrown over castle ramparts. |
| **1611** | Sentenced to life in solitary confinement. |
| **1614** | Dies bricked up behind a wall in her castle. |

# Charles I
## ◄ 1600–1649 ►
## KING OF ENGLAND

Charles I's tyrannical rule of Great Britain led to a civil war, his execution and the temporary eclipse of the monarchy.

Charles I was the second of the Stuart kings, inheriting from his father, James I (James VI of Scotland), an unpopular war against Spain. An authoritarian with a taste for luxury, the king's sympathies were known to lie with the High Church Party and he found little common ground with the Puritans who dominated the House of Commons. They refused to vote him the right to levy taxes, and when they questioned the conduct and expense of the war in 1626, he simply dissolved Parliament. Now at war with France as well, Charles ordered a tax which his own judges found illegal. So he sacked the chief justice and imprisoned over 70 noblemen who refused to pay.

In 1628, Charles recalled Parliament and was forced to sign a sweeping Petition of Rights in return for taxation. When a third parliament condemned his 'popish practices', he ordered it to adjourn. But when the speaker tried to rise to move the adjournment, he was physically restrained until three resolutions were passed condemning the king's actions. To Charles, this was treason and parliament remained closed for 11 years.

The king then tried to impose his High Church beliefs on Presbyterian Scotland. When this failed, he declared war on his Scots subjects. Parliament was recalled in April 1640 to raise funds for this. Instead it voiced numerous grievances and the king dissolved Parliament again within a month. But when the king's army was defeated by the Scots at Newburn, he summoned what was to be known as the Long Parliament in November 1640.

The new parliament condemned the king and ordered the arrest of his ministers. He tried to placate the Parliamentarians by signing the Triennial Act, which guaranteed that a parliament would be called at least once every three years. This failed to mollify the Parliamentarians and they executed the Earl of Strafford, the king's most trusted adviser, on 12 May 1641. Charles was forced to sign an act preventing Parliament being dissolved without its own consent. Then in November 1641, the House of Commons passed the Grand Remonstrance, listing everything Charles had done wrong since he had come to the throne.

When Ireland rebelled, Parliament, fearing that any army raised to put down the rebellion would be used against them, moved to take control of the military. Charles ordered the arrest of six Members of Parliament, but they escaped.

In June 1942, Parliament sent the king the Nineteen Proposals, demanding, again, Parliamentary control of the army, the ratification of government ministers and a say in Church policy. The king refused and began touring the country, trying to raise support. When on 20 August Charles raised his standard at Nottingham, this served as a formal declaration of war against Parliament.

Charles was defeated by the Parliamentarian forces under Oliver Cromwell. While in captivity, the king managed to persuade the Scots to his cause, beginning a second Civil War, which ended with the defeat of the Scots in the Battle of Preston in 1648.

*Charles I, portrayed as emperor and Knight of St George, in a portrait by Anthony Van Dyck.*

The Parliamentarian New Model Army then demanded that the king be put on trial as 'the grand author of our troubles'. Charles was charged with treason and 'other high crimes against the realm of England'. But – as king – he refused to recognize that the court had any jurisdiction over him. The court, however, was of a different opinion: Charles was found guilty and beheaded in Whitehall on 30 January 1649.

# Life and Crimes

**1600**  Born 19 November in Dunfermline Palace, Fife.

**1603**  His father James VI of Scotland invited to become James I of England, uniting the two kingdoms.

**1625**  Succeeds his father as King of Great Britain and Ireland.

**1626**  Dissolves Parliament when it questions conduct of war with Spain; orders taxation: when this is judged illegal, sacks chief justice and imprisons those who refuse to pay.

**1628**  Adjourns Parliament for eleven years.

**1640**  Starts war with Scots; recalls Parliament; dissolves it after a month but, short of money, is forced to recall it again.

**1642**  Rejects Parliament's Nineteen Proposals; Civil War starts.

**1647**  Defeated; captured; rejects Parliamentary terms and comes to secret understanding with the Scots.

**1648**  Scots defeated at the battle of Preston.

**1649**  Tried and executed as a tyrant, traitor, murderer and public enemy on 30 January.

# Aurangzeb
## ◀ 1618–1707 ▶
## MUGHAL EMPEROR OF INDIA

The Mughal emperor Aurangzeb ruled a vast tract of what is now India and Pakistan. A passionate Muslim, he was intolerant of other religions. He removed the tax-free status that his great-grandfather Akbar had granted the Hindus, destroyed their temples, and crushed their vassal states, which had previously enjoyed semi-independent status. In 1675, he alienated the Sikhs by executing the Sikh Guru Tegh Bahadur for refusing to become a Muslim, starting a feud that lasted for centuries. Other religious dissidents were also summarily executed.

Aurangzeb came to power by imprisoning his father Shah Jahan and executing the Crown Prince Dara Shukoh and two other brothers. In the Mughal tradition it is customary for sons to overthrow their father and for brothers to fight to the death among themselves to take over. Aurangzeb's mother was Mumtaz Mahal for whom the Taj Mahal was built.

Even before he became emperor in 1658, he had led troops against the Uzbeks and Persians with distinction and had served two terms as viceroy of the Deccan provinces, reducing the two Muslim Deccan kingdoms to near subjugation.

Reigning for the next 49 years, he expanded his kingdom into the far south of India through the Deccan plain. Within his empire he enforced strict religious laws, razing the shrines and temples of other faiths and destroying works of art in case they were worshipped as idols. Words from the Koran were also removed from coins, lest they be touched by unbelievers.

His reign was marked by almost constant warfare and rebellions that had to be put down. A Sunni, he persecuted Shias and Sufis along with non-Muslims. One of his greatest enemies was the Maratha chief Shivaji, who twice plundered the great port of Surat. Once defeated, Shivaji was called to Agra to be given imperial rank, but he fled to the Deccan where he established an independent Maratha kingdom

When Shivaji died in 1680, his son Sambhaji took over and the Mughal-Maratha Wars began. Sambhaji was captured in 1689 and executed with some cruelty. His wife and son were taken into captivity, but his half-brother Rajaram pulled back into the Tamil country in the southeast and frustrated Mughal advances into the Deccan until 1700.

Aurangzeb's religious intolerance caused internal dissent which weakened his realm. The vastness of the empire strained its army, its bureaucracy and its economy, and when Aurangzeb died in 1707, the empire became an easy target for invasion. First Maratha bounced back, forming its own empire on what was formerly Mughal territory, only to be overtaken by the British.

# Life and Crimes

**1618** Born 3 November in Dhod, Malwa, India.

**1636** Becomes viceroy in the Deccan.

**1646** Fights the Uzbeks and Persians.

**1658** Seizes the throne.

**1675** Arrests and executes Tegh Bahadur for refusing to become a Muslim.

**1679** Taxes non-Muslims.

**1686** Conquers Deccan kingdoms of Bijapur and Golconda.

**1689** Destroys kingdom of Maratha.

**1707** Dies 3 March.

# Peter the Great

## ◀ 1672–1725 ▶

## TSAR OF RUSSIA

Peter was just four years old when his father Tsar Alexis died. The son of a second marriage, he was strong and healthy, unlike his half-brother Fyodor III who succeeded.

When Fyodor died childless in 1682, infighting broke out between the families of Alexis's two wives. Peter was named tsar, but the Moscow musketeers – the streltsy – rebelled, forcing him to rule jointly with his feeble-minded half-brother Ivan V under the regency of Ivan's 25-year-old sister Sophia. But in August 1689 Peter and his guardian Prince Boris Golitsyn succeeded in overthrowing Sophia and banishing her.

Between 1694 and 1697 Peter set about improving Russia's maritime position. He fought the Crimean Tartars and took control of Azov from the Turks, giving Russia access to crucial trading ports on the Black Sea.

He then undertook a European tour to secure allies against the Ottoman empire, visiting Germany, Holland and Britain, but had to return when

*Peter the Great beheads a rebel streltsy noble, as the others are forced to look on and drink to their comrade's extinction.*

the streltsy staged another rebellion. Crushing it, he executed thousands of streltsy, beheading many of them himself. He also got Sophia out of the way by forcing her into a convent, along with his wife the beautiful Eudoxia, of whom he had tired.

Determined to modernize Russia, he replaced the Julian calendar with the Gregorian one, which had now been adopted across most of Europe. Because Europeans were clean-shaven, Peter introduced a beard tax in an effort to force the boyars – the traditional Russian nobility – to follow suit. This was not a popular move.

Next Peter sought an outlet to the Baltic. He conscripted 32,000 men and attacked the Swedes at Livonia in August 1700. However, he was soundly defeated at the battle of Narva that November by the Swedish king, Charles XII, losing over 15,000 men to the Swedes' 650. But he did not give up. Employing expert advisers he defeated the Swedes at Erestfer and Hummelshof in 1702. Occupying the Neva valley, he built St Petersburg – his 'window on the West' – on a frozen marsh on the Gulf of Finland.

In the summer of 1704, he besieged Narva, taking it on 21 August. The Swedes reacted by invading Russia, pushing Peter all the way back to the central Ukraine. Once again the Russian winter got the better of the invaders and the Swedes were obliterated at the Battle of Poltava.

In 1711, he attacked the Turks in Moldavia. Then in 1714, he destroyed the Swedish fleet near Hangö, giving Russia a permanent hold on the Baltic.

Peter did transform Russia, building arms factories, military schools, canals and shipyards using a workforce of over a million conscripts. When the people rebelled against a three-fold increase in taxes to fund his adventures, he cracked down with executions, floggings, mutilation and permanent exile to Siberia. The clergy were tortured to reveal the secrets of the confessional and murdered if they refused. Even Peter's own son Alexis rebelled against him. When the conspiracy was uncovered Alexis fled abroad, but was forcibly returned, imprisoned and tortured to death.

In 1721, Peter had himself named Emperor of all the Russias, seized control of the Church as patriarch and spent the next two years fighting the Persians and pushing back Russia's Asian frontier. He died on 8 February 1725, having changed the face of Russia.

# Life and Crimes

**1672** Born 30 May in Moscow.

**1676** Father Tsar Alexis dies, causing rivalry between the families of his two wives.

**1682** Peter named tsar, but forced to rule jointly with Ivan V under regency of Sophia.

**1689** Ousts Sophia.

**1694–1695** Leads military expedition to White Sea.

**1695–1696** Fights Crimean Tartars; takes Azov.

**1697** Tours Europe.

**1698** Returns to put down rebellion; sends Sophia to a nunnery.

**1699** Drafts army of 32,000.

**1700** Attacks Swedes; defeated at battle of Narva.

**1702** Defeats Swedes at Erestfer and Hummelshof.

**1703** Founds St Petersburg on 16 May.

**1704** Takes Narva.

**1707** Sweden invades.

**1709** Obliterates Swedes at battle of Poltava.

**1711** Attacks Turks in Moldavia.

**1714** Destroys Swedish fleet and takes control of Baltic.

**1721** Baltic states ceded to Russia; named Emperor of all the Russias.

**1722–1723** Fights Persians.

**1725** Dies 8 February.

# Nadir Shah

## ◀ 1688–1747 ▶

## RULER OF PERSIA

When informed that paradise was a peaceful place, the Persian warrior Nadir Shah remarked: 'How then can there be any delights there?'

After serving a local chieftain, Nadir rebelled and became head of an army of bandits. Throwing his support behind Tahmasp II, heir to the Iranian throne lost to the Afghans four years earlier, Nadir pushed the Afghans out of Persia. When Tahmasp lost to the Turks, ceding Georgia and Armenia, Nadir deposed him, put his son on the throne with himself as regent, then took back everything Tahmasp had lost. The mere threat of warfare by Nadir forced the tsar to hand over the Caspian provinces and, in 1736, Nadir deposed Tahmasp's son and took the throne himself.

Moving into the Arabian peninsula, Nadir took Bahrain and Oman. Then, after taking Kabul, he marched through the Khyber Pass, defeating the Mughal armies at Karnal. He sacked Delhi, massacring thousands, then returned to Iran with the Peacock Throne and the Koh-I-noor diamond.

He tried to force the Shi'ite Muslims in Iran to become Sunnis, and attacked the Uzbeks and Turks once more. But his people grew tired of the cost and loss of life of his constant wars, and their protests soon began to be heard. Suspecting that his eldest son had turned against him, Nadir ordered him to be blinded and he put down popular uprisings with torture and execution. When he ordered the execution of all Persian officers in the army, however, the army decided that this was too much, and turned on him. Nadir was finally assassinated on 19 June 1747.

## Life and Crimes

**1688**  Born Nadr Qoli Beg on 22 October at Kobhan, Safavid, Iran.

**1726** Leads army of bandits in support of Tahmasp II.

**1729** Drives Afghans out of Persia.

**1733** Deposes Tahmasp; becomes regent to his son; attacks Turks.

**1735** Takes Caspian states from Russia without a fight.

**1736** Deposes Tahmasp's son, taking the throne himself.

**1739** Defeats Mughals at battle of Karnal; sacks Delhi.

**1741** Orders blinding of his own son.

**1743** Renews attacks on Turks.

**1746** Defeats Turks at Yerevan.

**1747** Assassinated 19 June at Fathabad.

# THE NAPOLEONIC ERA

By the 18th century, tyranny took on a more ideological gloss, not least in the quest for modernization. Clearly an absolute ruler could make changes more easily by brooking no opposition. Even those who sought to expand their empires did so, not for personal aggrandisement but to spread the benefits of civilization, or so they said. Others in Latin America set off down the path of tyranny while throwing off the imperial yolk. The French Revolution threw up dictators determined to spread liberty, equality and fraternity by force and bloodshed. They established a pattern that would be followed in the 20th century with disastrous consequences.

# Catherine the Great
## ◀ 1729–1796 ▶
### TSARINA OF RUSSIA

Catherine the Great ruled Russia from 1762 to 1796. Like all the tsars, she was an absolute ruler and built on the reforms of Peter the Great to establish Russia as a great power. Although she is now better known for – the somewhat exaggerated – tales of her sexual appetites than her political excesses, her sexual life and her political life were inextricably linked.

Catherine was born on 2 May 1729 in the Prussian city of Stettin, now Szcezecin in Poland. At 16 she was married to her 17-year-old cousin Peter, the German-born grandson of Peter the Great and heir to the throne of Russia. However, Peter was an alcoholic, impotent and feeble-minded.

For six years, Catherine contented herself with horse riding and voracious reading. But the Empress Elizabeth, Peter's aunt and Russia's reigning monarch, wanted her to have children to continue the Romanov line. So on an out-of-the-way island in the Baltic, Elizabeth arranged for Catherine, who was still a virgin, to spend time with Sergei Saltykov, a Russian nobleman and accomplished womanizer.

After one night with Saltykov, Catherine could not get enough sex. After two miscarriages, she gave birth to Paul, who was whisked away by Elizabeth and presented to the Russian people as heir to the throne.

Soon after, Catherine's husband Peter underwent an operation which corrected a malformation of his penis and made him potent, and he began taking a string of mistresses. However, he does not seem to have had sex with Catherine who by this time had had a second child by a young Polish nobleman named Count Stanislaw Poniatowski.

'I do not know how it is my wife becomes pregnant,' Peter said.

He soon found out when he caught Count Poniatowski leaving their country home in disguise. He accused the count of sleeping with his wife. Naturally, Poniatowski denied it. Peter had Catherine dragged out of bed, and he and Poniatowski were then forced to have supper with Peter and his latest mistress. Afterwards, Poniatowski was sent back to Poland in disgrace.

Catherine replaced him with an officer in the Horse Guards, Count Grigori Orlov, who soon got her pregnant. She managed to conceal her belly under the huge hooped dresses which were then in fashion. When she felt the child coming, one of her servants set his own house on fire to distract Peter, who never could resist a good fire. She had three children with Orlov, always handing them over to servants as soon as they were born, and only introducing them to the royal nursery once no one could really be sure to whom they belonged.

Catherine's infidelity drove Peter crazy and, when he came to the throne in 1761, he was determined to divorce her. But Peter was deeply unpopular. He made no effort to conceal his hatred of Russia and his love of all things German, and worse still, he worshipped Frederick II of Prussia, with whom Russia was currently at war. After just six months on the throne, Peter concluded a peace treaty with Frederick and started planning a disastrous war against Denmark.

Although Catherine had been born in Germany too, she was much more popular than her husband. Dressed in a lieutenant's uniform she rode to St Petersburg, where Count Orlov was stationed, with the army behind her, and proclaimed herself Empress in Kazan Cathedral. Peter was arrested. He abdicated, but was murdered anyway eight days later by Orlov's brother Aleksei. Catherine then installed her old lover Stanislaw Poniatowski on the throne of Poland and went to war with Turkey.

Catherine refused to marry Orlov, preferring to preserve the Romanov dynasty. He got his own back by seducing every attractive woman who came to court. He became a political liability when he bungled peace negotiations with the Ottomans, prolonging the war with Turkey. He capped that by seducing Catherine's 13-year-old cousin. Catherine kicked him out and he died mad, haunted, so he claimed, by the ghost of the murdered Emperor Peter.

The hardships imposed by the war caused discontent, added to by an outbreak of plague. The result was an uprising led by Yemelyan Pugachov, a Don Cossack who claimed to be the dead emperor Peter the Great. He was preparing to march on Moscow when the war with Turkey was won and Catherine was able to turn her full force against him. Pugachov was captured and beheaded, but the rebellion had left Catherine in fear of her people. Abandoning her liberal ideas, she tightened the grip of serfdom,

*Catherine the Great: rumours of her sexual predilections are grossly exaggerated.*

imposing it on the Ukraine where it had not been in operation before. By the end of her reign there was hardly a peasant in the country who was free.

Much of this was done under the influence of cavalry officer Prince Grigori Potemkin, who had distinguished himself in the war with Turkey. When he met Catherine, they had fallen instantly in love, infuriating Orlov's brother, who had Potemkin so badly beaten that he had lost an eye. When Catherine's affair with Orlov ended, she planned to replace him with Potemkin but, after swearing his loyalty, Potemkin retired to a monastery. He refused to return to court until Catherine sent away all her other favourites.

For two years they had an intense affair. But when Potemkin began to put on weight Catherine turned to younger men, although Potemkin retained his position at court, and Catherine referred to him as her 'husband'. Meanwhile, to retain some control, he hand-picked handsome cavalry officers as lovers for her. Candidates were first examined for symptoms of syphilis, and then had their virility tested by one of Catherine's ladies-in-waiting.

At least 13 officers passed this exhaustive selection procedure. They were installed in special apartments below Catherine's, connected to hers by a private staircase. One thousand roubles would be waiting for them there. If a candidate proved satisfactory and a repeat performance was required, the 'emperor of the night' would be promoted to the rank of adjutant general and given a salary of 12,000 roubles a month plus expenses. One of her lovers said that they considered themselves 'kept girls'. When she was finished with a lover, he would receive a handsome golden handshake which in one case amounted to an estate with 4,000 serfs.

Potemkin's influence continued undiminished. He organized the annexation of the Crimea from the Turks in 1783 and extended Russian territory along the shore of the Black Sea. Catherine then announced her intention of taking Constantinople.

However, at 60, Catherine fell in love with 22-year-old Platon Zubov and the ambitious Zubov became Potemkin's rival for power. After Potemkin died in 1791, Catherine went on to annex the western Ukraine and wipe Poland off the map, dividing it between Russia, Prussia and Austria. In all, she added 200,000 square miles of territory to Russia.

The myth persists that Catherine died when she declared that no man could satisfy her, and tried sex with a horse. The horse, it was said, was lowered on to her by crane. The crane broke and she was crushed to death. There is no evidence to support this scandalous tale, probably an invention of the French, the sworn enemies of Catherine and her fellow aristocrats. She died at the age of 67, two days after suffering a massive stroke: no equine involvement has ever been reliably established.

# Life and Crimes

**1729**  Born 2 May in Stettin, Prussia.

**1745**  Marries heir to the Russian throne.

**1761**  Her husband becomes tsar.

**1762**  Proclaims herself empress; husband abdicates and is murdered; takes over lands and serfs belonging to the Church.

**1764**  Installs her lover Stanislaw Poniatowski on the Polish throne.

**1767**  Writes liberal constitution but fails to put it into practice.

**1768**  Goes to war with Turkey.

**1774**  Crushes Cossack rebellion.

**1775**  Tightens the grip of serfdom.

**1783**  Annexes Crimea.

**1792**  Annexes western Ukraine.

**1795**  Dismembers Poland.

**1796**  Dies 6 November at Tsarskoye Selo (now Pushkin) near St Petersburg.

# Louis XVI

◀ 1754–1793 ▶

## KING OF FRANCE

Louis XVI was the last of a long line of tyrants. His grandfather Louis XIV was the very apotheosis of an absolute monarch, styling himself the 'Sun King' and living in great splendour in Versailles while his people starved. Economic conditions in France had not improved when Louis XVI came to the throne in 1774 at the age of twenty.

Louis's chief financial officer, a man named Anne Robert Jacques Turgot, tried to reform the country's finances. He sought to replace the corvée – a feudal levy paid in labour – with a monetary tax, to ease the guild laws to encourage manufacturing and to cut the expenses of the monarchy. Turgot's reforms were rejected by the regional parlements, which consisted largely of the nobility who would have to pay the new tax. When the reforms failed, Turgot was dismissed.

The Seven Years War and Louis' backing of the American rebels nearly bankrupted the country. Over one half of the country's budget was dedicated to paying off the debt. Tax collection was catastrophically disorganized. It varied from region to region and was undertaken by private businessmen who took a handsome profit. In the absence of a central exchequer, hundreds of government offices disbursed money, rendering it virtually impossible for anyone to have any idea of how much was coming in or going out. The accelerating financial crisis quickly caused inflation and, by 1789, over 80 per cent of an average peasant's household income went on purchasing bread alone and unemployment in many parts of France had reached over 50 per cent. And all the while Louis and his wife Marie-Antoinette continued to flaunt their extravagant lifestyle in front of the very people whose poverty they perpetuated.

Louis tried to get his tax reform through the regional parlements again. They insisted that he called a national Estates-General for the first time since 1614. The assembly was made up of three Estates. The First Estate represented the nobility; the Second Estate the clergy and the Third Estate the majority of people, whose economic power had increased considerably since the seventeenth century. As no adjustment had been made between the power of the estates, the Third Estate was easily out-voted, so its representatives walked out and formed the National Assembly which demanded a new constitution.

As the situation in the country deteriorated with many regions now facing starvation, Louis was forced to publicly recognize the Assembly, while he mustered troops to dissolve it. Fearing that the Assembly was going to be suppressed, rioters took to the streets of Paris and, on 14 July 1789 they stormed the Bastille – the fortress prison that was a symbol of Bourbon oppression – beginning the French Revolution. On that day, Louis wrote in his diary the single word: 'Rien' – 'Nothing happened'.

Events quickly overtook him. On 6 October, the king and his family were removed from Versailles and held under house arrest in the Tuileries palace in Paris. Louis was forced to accept a constitution limiting his powers. In June 1791 he tried to escape but was caught on the German border. He was returned to Paris, where he remained the constitutional king for another year. The outbreak of war with Austria in April 1792 made people suspicious of Marie-Antoinette, who was an Austrian princess, and probably responsible for Louis' worst excesses. While Louis began plotting to reverse the revolution, the National Assembly abolished the office of king, declaring France to be a republic. A mob stormed the Tuileries on 10 August 1792, taking the king and queen prisoner. They were put on trial for treason in front of the National Assembly and found guilty by a vote of 361 to 288, with 72 abstentions. Louis was guillotined in front of a cheering crowd in the Place de la Revolution – now the Place de la Concorde – on 21 January 1793. Marie-Antoinette followed him to the scaffold on 16 October. Their son, named Louis XVII by French aristocrats in exile, died in prison.

## Life and Crimes

**1754** Born 23 August in Versailles.

**1770** Marries Austrian princess Marie-Antoinette.

**1774** Ascends to the throne on 10 May.

**1789** Storming of the Bastille.

**1791** Forced to become constitutional monarch; attempts to escape.

**1792** Tuileries stormed; royal family imprisoned.

**1793** Guillotined in the Place de la Revolution in Paris, 21 January.

# Maximilien Robespierre
### ◀ 1758–1794 ▶
## REVOLUTIONARY FRENCH LEADER

Leader of the Committee of Public Safety, Maximilien Robespierre was responsible for the Reign of Terror that followed the French Revolution.

Born the son of a lawyer in Arras, he won a scholarship to study law in Paris. He was admired for his abilities, but his austerity and dedication won him few personal friends. Returning to his native Arras, he practised law and gained a reputation for advocacy. A Jacobin, he came under the influence of Jean Jacques Rousseau's theories of democracy and deism, and Robespierre's emphasis on virtue – which in his mind meant civic morality – earned him the epithet 'the Incorruptible'. He even slept with a copy of Rousseau's *Social Contract* at his side.

Known for his neat dress and frugal ways, Robespierre was chosen to represent the city of Arras at the Estates-General conceded by Louis XVI in 1789 and oversaw the writing of the new constitution that was forced on the king. After Louis XVI fled in 1791, Robespierre called for his trial and, at that trial, he called for Louis' death. In 1792, he was elected to the Commune of Paris and represented the capital at the National Convention. After the king was executed, Robespierre called for further excesses. In 1793, he got a decree passed indicting twenty-nine leading moderates who had accused him of fostering a dictatorship. Robespierre was unrepentant. What was needed now, he said, was 'a single will'. That will was to be his.

Taking his place on the twelve-man Committee of Public Safety, he called for a revolutionary militia to combat counter-revolutionaries and grain hoarders. Massacres followed. The fledgling republic found itself embroiled in a civil war and under attack from outside by Britain, Austria, Spain, Portugal, Prussia, Russia, Sardinia and Naples. On 5 September 1793 – 9 Thermidor, Year 1 in the Revolutionary calendar – the revolutionaries issued a decree making 'terror' the order of the day. The enemies of the Revolution – nobles, churchmen and those suspected of hoarding food and private property – were to be eliminated. There followed a wave of atrocities known as the Reign of Terror.

The first plan was to send the revolutionary army from Paris out into the countryside with a mobile guillotine. But Robespierre, who now headed the all-powerful Committee of Public Safety, wanted an army of half-a-million men to do the job and introduced conscription.

On 17 September – 21 Thermidor – the Committee passed the Law of Suspects, which allowed them to arrest and execute anyone suspected of anti-revolutionary views.

'A river of blood will now divide France from its enemies,' rejoiced Robespierre.

The Revolution was a product of the age of reason and, in Robespierre's eyes, organized religion was the enemy. The Committee sent agents out across the country to dechristianize the population. Churches and cemeteries were vandalized. The Bishop of Paris was forced to resign and Notre Dame was deconsecrated and renamed the Temple of Reason.

Lyon had rebelled against the Jacobins, but on 9 October, after a bloody bombardment, the revolutionaries retook the city and renamed it Ville-Affranchie – Liberated Town. The houses of the rich were demolished and twenty to thirty rebels executed. Suspecting that the locals were being too lenient on their own, a revolutionary zealot named Mathieu Parein was sent to handle the situation. He ordered that those who had an income of thirty thousand livres or more had to hand it over immediately and that all vestiges of religion be obliterated. Houses were searched and mass executions began.

The guillotine became overworked. On 11 Nivôse, according the scrupulous accounts the Jacobins kept, thirty-two heads were severed in twenty-five minutes. A week later, twelve heads were severed in just five minutes and the residents of the rue Lafont where the guillotine was set up kept complaining about the blood overflowing from the drainage ditch that ran under the scaffold.

Mass shootings took place. As many as sixty prisoners were tied in a line with ropes and shot with cannons. Those who were not killed outright were finished off with bayonets, sabres and rifles. The chief butcher, an actor named Dorfeuille, wrote to Paris boasting that he had killed 113 Lyonnais in a single day. Three days later he butchered 209 and he promised that another four or five hundred would 'expiate their crimes with fire and shot'. This was an underestimate. By the time the killing had stopped, 1,905 were dead – and the victims were not restricted to the rich, the aristocratic and the clergy. The unemployed were also liquidated, along with anyone the Revolutionary Tribunal decided was a 'fanatique'.

Marseilles – now Ville-Sans-Nom (Town Without Name) – was similarly purged. After an insurrection in Vendée, the local agent wrote to the Committee of Public Safety in Paris describing their reprisals.

'There is no more Vendée, citizens,' he said. 'It has just perished under our free sword along with its women and children. I have just buried it in the marshes and mud of Savenay. Following the orders you gave me I have crushed children under the feet of horses and massacred women who at least will give birth to no more brigands. I have no prisoners with which to reproach myself.'

The name Vendée was changed to Vengé – Avenged.

Two hundred prisoners were executed in Angers in December alone; two thousand at Saint-Florent, and at Pont-de-Cé and Avrillé, three to four thousand were shot in one long, relentless slaughter. At Nantes the guillotine was so overworked that a new method of execution, known as 'vertical deportation', was developed. A flat-bottomed barge would be holed below the waterline, then a plank nailed over the hole to keep the boat temporarily afloat. Prisoners were put on the barge with their hands and feet tied. The barge would be taken out into the middle of the Loire where the executioner would pull out the plank and jump to safety on board a boat alongside. The barge would then go down taking the prisoners with it. Anyone attempting to escape drowning would be slashed with a sabre.

At first this form of execution was reserved for clerics and was known as a 'republican baptism'. Later the 'national bath' was more widely used. Prisoners were often stripped of their clothes first. Young men and young women were sometimes tied together naked and given a 'republican marriage'.

The revolutionary army spread out across the country looking for sedition. They would slaughter men, women and children they suspected of harbouring anti-Jacobin sympathies. Crops were also burned, farm animals slaughtered, barns and cottages demolished and woods torched. Any town or village that had entertained anti-Jacobin troops would be razed. Terrorists planned to put arsenic in wells and enquiries were made of a well-known chemist about the possibilities of developing poison gas.

Twelve infernal columns were sent to 'pacify' the countryside by killing everyone in the path. Women were raped, children killed, both mutilated. Entire families were found swimming in their own blood. One impeccable republican lost three of his sons plus his son-in-law on the first visit of the Jacobins. They returned to massacre his remaining son, his wife and their 15-year-old daughter. To save ammunition, General Cordeiller ordered his men to use the sabre instead of guns.

At Gonnord, General Crouzat forced 200 old people, along with mothers and children, to kneel in front of a pit they had dug. They were shot so they fell into the grave. Some tried to make a break for it, but were struck down by the hammer of a local mason. Thirty children and two women were buried alive when earth was shovelled into the pit.

In the Loire Valley, around a quarter of a million people were killed – that is a third of the population of the region, and that figure does not include those who lost their lives in the revolution or during the subsequent wars fighting on the republican side.

Although Robespierre condemned the massacres occurring in the provinces, he was master of his own bloodbath in Paris. When he made a speech on 5 February 1794, calling for the consolidation of democracy and the peaceful reign of constitutional laws, his Revolutionary Tribunal in Paris had already convicted and executed 238 men and 31 women, and a further 5,434 were in prison in Paris awaiting trial.

Here too the guillotine was overworked. A prostitute was executed for expressing royalist sentiments – she had merely complained that trade had dropped off since the Revolution. Following her to the scaffold was the one-time playmate of Mozart, Marie-Antoinette, Queen of France. Entire families were guillotined, the older members being forced to watch the younger being executed while awaiting their turn. When one prisoner stabbed himself to death in front of the Revolutionary Tribunal, the court ordered that his corpse be guillotined anyway. Revolutionary justice was not to be cheated.

The Revolution then began to consume its own. Anyone who opposed Robespierre was sentenced to 'look through the republican window'

– that is, put his head through the frame of the guillotine. When the great hero of the Revolution Georges Danton tried to call a halt to the Terror, he too was arrested and sent to be 'shaved by the national razor'. Meanwhile Robespierre backtracked on the Revolution's avowed atheism. The dechristianizers, who Robespierre now viewed as immoral, paid for this sea-change on Robespierre's part with their lives. He then instituted the Festival of the Supreme Being, in which he took the leading role. This was not a return to belief in God, he explained – Nature was the 'Supreme Being'. But many people wondered whether Robespierre really thought that the 'Supreme Being' was in fact Robespierre himself.

Robespierre was a prig. He saw himself as a missionary of virtue and believed he was using the guillotine as an instrument for the moral improvement of the nation. New crimes of 'slandering patriotism', 'seeking to inspire discouragement', 'spreading false news', 'depraving morals', 'corrupting the public conscience' and 'impairing the purity and energy of the revolutionary government' were introduced. To speed the course of justice, those accused were allowed no defence counsel and no witnesses could be called. The jury was made up of good citizens who had to come to a fair and unbiased judgement without being distracted by such trifles. There were only two possible outcomes: acquittal or death. Which usually meant death. Robespierre himself coined the slogan: 'Clemency is parricide'. Executions jumped from five a day in the new revolutionary month of Germinal to twenty-six in Messidor.

However, things had been going well for the French army and the danger from abroad had eased, and some Republicans began to doubt the need for such draconian measures. Anyone against this new Revolutionary justice must have something to hide, Robespierre argued, and promptly had them all investigated. Robespierre was so busy organizing the persecution that he did not realize that behind his back, leading Revolutionaries were mocking his cult of the Supreme Being.

On 26 July 1794 – 8 Thermidor, Year II – Robespierre made a speech calling for 'more virtue' and his supporters called for his enemies to be sent 'à la guillotine'. But the next day, critics pointed out that Robespierre had departed from protocol. Instead of speaking for the collective leadership, he had made a speech in his own name. Robespierre was lost for words at this accusation. In the silence a voice piped up: 'See, the blood of Danton chokes him.'

Quickly his opponents moved against him. They knew if they did not, they would soon face the guillotine. Robespierre and his supporters were arrested on 27 July – 9 Thermidor. He could hardly ask for clemency. He tried to shoot himself, but missed, shattering his jaw. Summarily tried, he went to the scaffold before a cheering mob in the Place de la Revolution the following morning. A fastidious little man, he went to his death covered in blood after the executioner pulled off the paper bandage that was holding his jaw together, to give the blade an unimpeded fall. Robespierre yelped in pain, only to be silenced by the falling blade.

During the Reign of Terror, over and above those who were slaughtered in the countryside, at least 300,000 people were arrested; 17,000 were officially executed, and many more died in prison or without trial.

## Life and Crimes

**1758**  Born 6 May in Arras.
**1789**  Chosen to represent Arras at the National Assembly in Versailles.
**1791**  Oversees writing of constitution; calls for trial of Louis XVI.
**1792**  Calls for execution of Louis XVI.
**1793**  Insigates Reign of Terror.
**1794**  Executed 28 July in Paris.

# Dr José Gaspar Rodríguez Francia
### ◄ 1766–1840 ►

## DICTATOR OF PARAGUAY

When Paraguay declared its independence from Spain and deposed the governor Don Bernardo Velasco in 1811, the only native Paraguayan in the country qualified to sit on the junta which was hastily formed in order to run the country was Dr José Gaspar Rodríguez Francia. Born in Asunción in 1766, Francia was the son of a Brazilian army officer who had come to Paraguay to grow tobacco. A francophile, he changed his name from the Portuguese França or Franza to Francia – the Spanish for France – and claimed French descent. After a couple of years at school under the Jesuits, he was sent to study theology at the University of Cordoba, over the river in what is now Argentina.

Although Francia took no part in the split from Spain – and was probably against it – at Somellera's suggestion, he was picked to sit on the junta. As the other two members knew nothing of government and the law, it was left to Francia to write a constitution. It ran to just four lines. When it was ratified by a hastily convened congress, Paraguay became the first independent republic in South America.

Francia soon found the two gold-braided generals who were his companions on the junta tiresome – largely because they did not instantly agree with everything he said. So he withdrew, leaving the government paralysed. Back in the countryside he stirred up discontent among the landowners, not a hard thing to do as Buenos Aires was at war with Spain and the Parana river, essentially the only way for goods to get in and out of Paraguay, was closed. He also ingratiated himself with the local Guaraní indians by treating those of Spanish blood with ostentatious contempt. Soon he was seen as the coming man.

When the junta in Buenos Aires sent a diplomat to Asunción to invite Paraguay to join the confederation, Francia seized his moment. He put out the word that the Argentines were attempting by diplomacy what they had failed to do by force in an earlier invasion. Although in Francia's absence the junta had been expanded to five, they were still all Spaniards and the people did not trust them to put the interests of Paraguay first. They had no choice but to recall Francia. His price was to be allowed to rule alone. He first became consul, then Perpetual Dictator of Paraguay, known informally as 'El Supremo'. Francia's coup was not entirely unopposed. The troops under Yegros rebelled. Cavallero intervened to restore order. Both were imprisoned. Cavallero strangled himself in prison in 1821; Yegros was executed.

Don Pedro Somellera, a fellow graduate of the University of Cordoba and Dr Francia's lifelong acquaintance, was arrested even though he had got Francia onto the junta in the first place. He was imprisoned along with his brother Benigno and the former governor Velasco. Somellera was held incommunicado, but noticed that his cell door was often left open and he was fed information that a counter-revolution was being planned to restore Velasco to the governorship. On the morning of 29 September 1814, soldiers took to the streets. But this was no counter-revolution; it was a trap. Those who rallied to their cause were shot down and hung up from gallows, while the soldiers who had seemingly led the counter-revolution paraded under the gibbet, shouting patriotic slogans. With this simple ruse Francia got rid of any opposition. Somellera, knowing Francia well, had avoided falling into the trap and was allowed to leave the country. Velasco died in prison.

Francia immediately instituted a reign of terror, imprisoning on trumped-up charges anyone who criticized him. It was said that the blacksmiths in Asunción could not forge shackles fast enough. Anyone who had previously held political office in the country was arrested and their property seized, and the houses where Francia fancied that plots were being hatched were burnt down.

He began a police force and set up a system of spying so effective that it was said he even knew the thoughts of the dying. Brother informed against brother; son against father; servant against master; husband against wife. Prisoners had no idea what they had been imprisoned for. No one dared ask. Some people were simply arrested and held until a ransom was paid, though they were rarely released even then. Few emerged from Francia's prisons. Prisoners were left there, ill-fed, unwashed, unkempt, with no medical attention until they died. Their relatives only knew they were still alive because they were permitted to send them food.

Francia also acted as chief executioner, issuing the bullets to his firing squads. But his men were not very good shots, and victims were often bayoneted to death. These executions always took place first thing in the morning. The banquillo – the stool where the condemned man sat – was set up outside Francia's window. He watched to make sure the deed was done and insisted that the body remained outside his window in the heat all day to make sure the victim was dead before the family were allowed to take it away.

Like other dictators, Francia was terrified of assassination. Even though the cigars he smoked were made by his sister, every one was carefully unrolled to see if it contained poison – his sister was not above suspicion because he had imprisoned her husband, along with his own brother and another brother-in-law, and he had a nephew executed. He checked all the ingredients of his meals and made his own yerba maté – the local narcotic known as 'Paraguayan Tea'. No one was permitted to come into his presence with even a cane in his hand or approach him within six paces, and their hands had to be kept well away from their sides. Francia himself was never without a loaded pistol and unsheathed sabre within easy reach. To guard again insurrection, no man in the army was promoted above the rank of captain. Nor did he trust his own government ministers, who were made to stand in the hot sun while he harangued them and were regularly imprisoned.

No one was allowed out on the street when Francia rode out with his escort. All shutters had to be closed along his route and orange trees, shrubs and other places of concealment were destroyed. Anyone caught in the streets had to prostrate themselves or risked being cut down by sabre. When his horse shied at a barrel outside a house, the owner was arrested.

Having been disappointed in love, Francia had little time for women. When the wife of one prisoner threw herself at Francia's feet and begged for her husband's release, Francia merely ordered another set of iron fetters be placed on his legs – and a further set every time she approached him. Her husband died in chains, along with a friend who also had the temerity to intercede on the poor man's behalf.

After 26 years in power, people began to believe that Francia was immortal. Then suddenly at the age of 74 he died. He caught a chill during a thunderstorm, which flooded his room, and took to his bed. When his doctor approached within six paces to examine him, Francia stabbed him with his sabre, then had a fit. The doctor called for help, but the sergeant of the guard refused to enter the room without direct orders from Dr Francia. The doctor explained that Francia was unconscious and unable to speak, but the sergeant said: 'Even so, if he comes round, he will punish me for disobedience'. As a consequence, Francia died.

For several days, no one dared believe that Francia was really dead. People were afraid that it might be a trap. They feared they were being enticed into expressing relief or joy – only to bring down the wrath of the miraculously undead El Supremo. Indeed, Paraguayans feared even to mention his name decades after his death. He was known simply as 'El Difunto' – the deceased.

Despite his contempt for religion, Dr Francia was laid out in state before the high altar of the cathedral in Asunción. A priest delivered a glowing eulogy which exhorted Paraguay to weep for the saviour of the country and described Francia as the 'guarantor of our national freedom'. Meanwhile, Francia's rule was praised by misguided Scottish radical Thomas Carlyle for its 'rigour'.

The night after the eulogy, Dr Francia's body disappeared from the cathedral, giving rise to the legend that the devil had claimed its own. It is thought the old Spanish families of Paraguay had taken revenge by throwing his cadaver into the river to be eaten by alligators.

## Life and Crimes

**1766** Born in Asunción, capital of Paraguay.

**1811** Joins three-man junta to govern newly independent Republic of Paraguay.

**1814** Seizes power as 'El Supremo' – 'Perpetual Dictator' and seals off the country from the outside world. Begins reign of terror against anyone even suspected of harbouring disloyal thoughts.

**1840** El Supremo finally becomes El Difunto.

# Napoleon Bonaparte
◄ 1769–1821 ►

## EMPEROR OF FRANCE

Both as first consul and self-made monarch, Napoleon would brook no opposition either within France or outside it. He reshaped his country and redrew the map of Europe, but his plan for world domination was foiled by the British.

He was born Napoleone Buonparte in Ajaccio, Corsica, soon after France had acquired the Mediterranean island from Genoa. At the age of ten, he was sent to military school in France where he found himself spurned as a foreigner. After graduating, he was commissioned as an artillery officer. He joined one of the revolutionary Jacobin Clubs in Grenoble and became involved in Corsican nationalism. In 1792, he was elected lieutenant colonel of the Ajaccio Volunteers, though after an unsuccessful action in nearby Sardinia, he fell out with the Corsican nationalists and had to flee to Marseilles with his family.

When the French Revolution broke out, he joined the republicans and helped drive the British out of their stronghold of Toulon. Having distinguished himself as an artillery officer, he was appointed artillery commander of the French Army of Italy. When Robespierre fell from power, Napoleon was briefly imprisoned. Released, he took a post in the Army of the Interior and saved the National Convention of 1795 with a 'whiff of grapeshot', firing a cannon on the crowds who opposed it.

As a reward, he was given command of the Army of Italy. He married Joséphine de Beauharnais, a widow with a notorious reputation, and changed his name to the French spelling – Napoleon Bonaparte. He defeated the Austrian and Sardinian armies, and marched on Turin. As a result, Nice and Savoy were ceded to France. The following year, he kicked the Austrians out of Italy completely. He then set up a number of puppet governments in the regions of Italy and looted the country's art treasures.

The Directory, which was then running France, asked him to invade England. Instead he proposed seizing Egypt as a stepping stone towards taking British India. On 19 May, he sailed with 35,000 troops, landing at

Alexandria. Agreeing to preserve Islamic law, he began restructuring the Egyptian government. But on 1 August 1798, the British, under Admiral Lord Nelson, destroyed his fleet in the Battle of the Nile, cutting him off from France, and in March the following year, he was defeated in Syria by a Turkish army under British command.

By this time the French Army was afflicted with the plague and in August Napoleon abandoned his men and fled back to France. Arriving on 14 October, he joined a coup d'état against the Directory on 9 November, taking power as one of three consuls. Under the new constitution, he became first consul, with the power to hire and fire members of the council of state, government officials and judges. He quickly consolidated his position to absolute ruler of France.

At that time, he was still a progressive. He improved education, encouraged industry, restructured the national debt and codified the law into the Code Napoléon. However, he re-introduced Roman Catholicism as the state religion, began a building programme using imperial Rome as its model and muzzled the press. He kept control using his secret police and a network of spies.

He beat the Austrians again at the Battle of Marengo, signed a peace treaty with Britain and, on 2 August 1802, was made first consul for life. But this was not enough. He annexed Savoy-Piedmont and occupied the Helvetic Republic in Switzerland and the Batavian Republic in The Netherlands. And he sent an army to retake Haiti which had seized its independence in a slave rebellion.

Meanwhile he sought to isolate France's traditional enemy Britain by restricting its trade. This brought war in May 1803 and Napoleon amassed an army of 170,000 ready to invade England. He used the discovery of an assassination plot to establish a hereditary dynasty. The Pope was summoned from Rome to crown him Emperor of France, but when the moment came Napoleon seized the crown and crowned himself, and then crowned Joséphine empress. The following year he had himself crowned King of Italy, and installed members of his own and Joséphine's family on to various European thrones.

His plans to invade England thwarted by the Royal Navy, Napoleon picked on the Austrians once more, defeating them outside Ulm between 25 September and 20 October. However, on 21 October, his fleet was soundly beaten by his old nemesis the Royal Navy at the Battle of Trafalgar (off south-west Spain), ending any possibility of invading Britain. On 13 November he took Vienna and on 2 December he finished off the Austrians at the battle of Austerlitz. The peace treaty added Venice and Dalmatia to Napoleon's Italian kingdom.

On 12 July 1806, he took the German states of the old Holy Roman Empire under his protection as the Confederation of the Rhine. To placate Britain, he offered to return Hanover to her control, provoking war with Prussia. But he defeated the Prussians decisively at Auerstadt and Jena on 14 October and took all the land between the Rhine and the Elbe.

War ensued with Russia, ending in a victory for Napoleon at Friedland, after which he took control of Poland. Now only the British stood between him and total domination of the European continent.

Unable to defeat the British at sea or invade, he tried a blockade. But the Portuguese – long-time allies of England – refused to comply. Napoleon marched on Portugal, but French troops in the Iberian Peninsula destabilized Spain. Napoleon forced King Charles IV and his son Ferdinand VII to abdicate on 5 and 6 May 1808 and Napoleon installed his brother Joseph Bonaparte on the Spanish throne. When Britain came to the aid of Portugal, embroiling Napoleon in the Peninsular War, Spain and Portugal's Latin American colonies seized the opportunity to declare their independence.

When the Empress Joséphine proved unable to give him a child, Napoleon divorced her and married Princess Marie-Louise, the daughter of the Emperor of Austria, on 2 April 1810. She bore him a son, who was named King of Rome, but never reigned. Within months of the wedding France and Austria were at war again. Defeat at the Battle of Wagram on 5–6 July lost Austria the provinces of Illyria and Galicia.

However, in the Peninsular War, Napoleon found himself losing to the Duke of Wellington. His response was to tighten the trade embargo. When Russia refused to comply Napoleon invaded, beating the Russians at the Battle of Borodino on 7 September 1812. A week later he arrived in Moscow to find it deserted and on fire. As the Russian winter closed in, Napoleon had no alternative but to retreat, under the constant harassment of Russian troops who were better able to cope with the appalling conditions. Again Napoleon fled, leaving his army to its fate: most of his soldiers never returned from Russia.

Back in Paris, Napoleon mustered a new army which beat the Russians and the Prussians at Lützen and Bautzen in May 1813, and defeated the Austrians again at Dresden in August. But he was defeated at the Battle of the Nations at Leipzig (16–19 October). Coalition forces invaded France the following year and on 13 March 1814, they took Paris. Napoleon abdicated on 6 April and was exiled to the island of Elba off Italy, then under British control.

He escaped, landing back in France, in Cannes, on 1 March 1815. The army rallied to him, but Napoleon now faced the combined forces of Britain, Prussia, Austria and Russia. He decided to do battle with his nemesis the Duke of Wellington first. They met at Waterloo on 18 June 1815. Napoleon delayed the attack that morning to allow the field to dry out for his cavalry, a move which would prove fatal, allowing Prussian reinforcements under Gerhard von Blücher to arrive in the nick of time and Napoleon was defeated.

This time he was exiled to St Helena, a remote British island in the South Atlantic, where he devoted himself to writing a self-serving memoir aimed at securing his legend. He died on 5 May 1821, ostensibly of stomach cancer, though he may have been poisoned either purposely or accidentally as arsenic was a popular medicine at the time. He was buried on St Helena. Remains – probably not his – were returned to France in 1842 and housed in a magnificent tomb in Les Invalides in Paris. Although Napoleon was honoured, he had been so reckless with the lives of young Frenchmen that the country remained under-populated for decades to come.

# Life and Crimes

**1769** Born 15 August in Ajaccio, Corsica.

**1779–1785** Attends military school in Brienne-le-Château and Paris.

**1791** Joins a revolutionary Jacobin Club.

**1792** Becomes lieutenant colonel of Ajaccio Volunteers.

**1793** Fights in Sardinia; family flees to Marseilles; drives British from Toulon, becoming national hero.

**1794** Becomes artillery commander in French Army in Italy; imprisoned 6 August to 14 September.

**1795** Gives Parisian crowds a 'whiff of grapeshot'.

**1796** Takes command of the Army of Italy; annexes Nice and Savoy; enters Milan.

**1797** Defeats Austrians after long siege at Mantua; advances on Vienna sending Austrians to the peace table.

**1798** Lands in Egypt; defeated by Nelson at the Battle of the Nile.

**1799** Defeated in Syria; returns to France; stages coup d'état; appointed consul.

**1800** Becomes first consul with dictatorial powers; defeats the Austrians at the Battle of Marengo.

**1802** Created first consul for life.

**1803** Prepares to invade England.

**1804** Crowns himself Emperor of France.

**1805** Crowned King of Italy; defeats Austrians at Ulm; defeated by Nelson at the Battle of Trafalgar.

**1806** Takes control of Germany.

**1807** Defeats Russia and takes control of Poland.

**1808** Installs his brother on the throne of Spain.

**1809** Defeats Austria at the Battle of Wagram, taking Illyria and Galicia.

**1812** Defeats Russians at the Battle of Borodino; enters Moscow to find it empty and on fire; forced to make disastrous retreat.

**1813** Defeated at the Battle of the Nations.

**1814** France invaded and Napoleon forced to abdicate; exiled on Elba.

**1815** Escapes; returns to France; defeated at Waterloo; exiled on St Helena.

**1821** Dies 5 May.

# Shaka

◄ c. 1787–1828 ►

## CHIEF OF THE ZULU

Born the illegitimate son of the Zulu chief Senszangakona, Shaka was driven out with his mother Nandi, a Langeni, which the Zulu considered an inferior clan. Even his name was an insult – 'iShaka' was an intestinal parasite thought to be responsible for menstrual irregularities, and said by Zulu elders to be the true cause of Nandi's pregnancy.

At 16, Shaka was taken under the protection of Dingiswayo, king of the Mtetwa, and trained in his army. When Senzangakona died, Shaka returned to the Zulu – numbering then just 1,500 – as their chief. Those who had driven him and his mother out ended up impaled on the sharpened stakes of their own kraal fences.

He reorganized his army, introducing the famous bulls' horns formation and training his men to run barefoot up to 50 miles a day. Insubordination resulted in instant death. He then set about destroying all the tribes around him, integrating any survivors into the Zulu nation which, within a year, had quadrupled in number. When Dingiswayo died, Shaka took over the Mtetwa Empire, introducing the scorched earth policy to Africa when he began the Mfecane ('the Crushing'), arbitrarily wiping out clans across the Natal plateau. The devastation was so complete that the Boer's Great Trek of the 1830s passed through an uninhabited landscape.

The Zulu nation grew to 250,000. With an army of 40,000 it occupied territory that stretched from the Cape Colony to modern-day Tanzania. In the creation of this empire, it is estimated that Shaka killed over two million people, often in mass executions.

In 1827, his mother died. In grief Shaka had over 7,000 Zulus killed. No crops were planted for a year and milk, a Zulu staple, was banned. Milch cows were slain so that calves could know what it felt like to lose a mother and pregnant women were slain with their husbands.

Enforced chastity had already dispirited Shaka's army. When they were sent further and further from home to find lands to conquer, they rebelled.

Two of Shaka's half-brothers, Mhlangana and Dingane, murdered him. He died begging his assassins for mercy. They buried him in an unmarked grave near the village of Stanger in Natal.

# Life and Crimes

**c.1787**  Born the son of Zulu chief and Langeni mother.

**1802**  Driven out with his mother.

**1810**  Joins the army of Dingiswayo, chief of the Mtetwa.

**1816**  Becomes chief of the Zulu; takes revenge for his expulsion.

**1817**  After the death of Dingiswayo, begins expansion of Zulu Empire.

**1820**  Begins the Mfecane (the Crushing) devastating Natal.

**1827**  Mother's death leaves him openly psychotic.

**1828**  Murdered by half-brothers.

# Juan Manuel de Rosas
### ◀ 1793–1877 ▶

## DICTATOR OF THE ARGENTINE CONFEDERATION

Rosas was born to a wealthy family who owned some of the largest cattle ranches on the pampas. When he acquired land of his own, he gathered around him an army of gauchos – the local cowboys – to protect his property from the Indians.

In 1820, the governor of Buenos Aires, Colonel Manuel Dorrego, appointed Rosas head of the provincial militia. When Dorrego fell from power in 1828, Rosas, a federalist, opposed the new governor Juan Lavalle. He reconvened the former legislature which elected him governor in 1829. For four years he fought other provinces that were unwilling to join the Argentine Confederation.

At the end of his three-year term of office Rosas stepped down. However his strong leadership had made him very popular. In 1835, he was invited to become governor again. He agreed, but only if he was given dictatorial powers. For the next 17 years, he ruled the country, using troops and his secret police to crush any opposition. Supporters were given lucrative jobs in the administration. Opposition newspapers were burned in public squares and anyone deemed a threat was purged. Rosas even ordered that his portrait should be hung in churches and public places to show that he had absolute authority.

To tighten his grip, Rosas also took over the judicial system. He would sit in judgement over cases, imposing sentences that included fines, service in the army, imprisonment, banishment or execution.

Anyone on the state payroll – from military officers, priests, to civil servants and teachers – were obliged to wear a red badge with the inscription 'Federation or Death'. Every male was required to sport a large moustache and sideburns – 'the federal look' – and all civilians were required to wear red. Public spending was slashed. Land was confiscated from indigenous peoples and anti-Federalist, and Rosas, a slave owner himself, sought to revive the slave trade.

In the end, armies from Brazil and Uruguay joined with Argentine dissidents under the command of Justo José de Urquiza, the powerful governor of the neighbouring province of Entre Rios, and defeated Rosas at the battle of Caseros in 1852. Rescued by the Royal Navy, Rosas was taken to England where he became a gentleman farmer in Hampshire. Meanwhile Urquiza laid the basis of a federal constitution and, in 1862, Argentina became a united country with Buenos Aires as its capital.

# Life and Crimes

**1793** Born 30 March in Buenos Aires.

**1820** Became head of provincial militia.

**1829** Elected governor of Buenos Aires 5 December.

**1831** The Argentine Confederation formed.

**1832** Retires from office.

**1835** Becomes dictator of the province of Buenos Aires.

**1848** Becomes dictator of the Argentine Confederation.

**1852** Defeated at battle of Caseros on 3 February.

**1877** Dies 14 March in Southampton, England.

# Francisco Solano López
### ◄ 1827–1870 ►
## DICTATOR OF PARAGUAY

Francisco Solano López was the son of Carlos López, the successor to Dr Francia as Paraguayan dictator – and he would be worse for the unfortunate Paraguayan nation than either of his predecessors. López Jnr was a life-long fan of another short man – Napoleon – and his favourite bedtime reading was *El Catecismo de San Alberto*, an account of the savage suppression of the insurrection of Tupac Amaru II, the last descendant of the Inca emperors, who, after being forced to witness the execution of his wife and sons, was mutilated, drawn, quartered and beheaded.

He was short, fat, ugly, barrel-chested and bandy-legged from learning to ride early in life. And like Carlos, he showed a predilection for extravagant uniforms, having them cut tight in a futile attempt to disguise his corpulence.

'His eyes, when pleased, had a mild expression; but when he was enraged the pupil seemed to dilate till it did not appear to be that of a human being, but rather a wild animal,' wrote Ambassador Washburn undiplomatically. 'He had, however, a gross animal look that was repulsive when in repose. His forehead was narrow and his head small, with the rear organs largely developed. His teeth were very much decayed, and so many of the front ones were gone as to render his articulation somewhat difficult and indistinct.'

Washburn concluded that Francisco made no effort to clean his teeth and said those that remained were unwholesome in appearance and as black as the cigar he kept permanently clenched between them. Washburn also described Francisco, whom he clearly had not taken to, as a 'licensed ravisher', one who had developed a taste for aristocratic virgins. Any that refused him would find their father and brothers jailed – few left Paraguayan prisons alive. One woman called Pancha Garmendia – known to all who saw her as the 'jewel of Asunción' – resisted as her father had already been killed by Dr Francia. Francisco had her kept in chains and beaten and raped daily for the remaining twenty-three years of her life.

Another resisted on the grounds that she was about to be married. On the eve of her wedding the naked and mutilated corpse of her fiancé was thrown through her front window, driving the unfortunate woman over the edge of madness.

Eventually, even his father Carlos could no longer stomach Francisco, and decided it might be wise for Francisco to leave the country for a bit, until the various scandals had died down. He gave Francisco money and sent him to Europe to buy a navy, despite the fact that Paraguay is landlocked and does not need a navy.

*Francisco Solano López, in the favoured outfit for despots, a military uniform, complete with decorations to which he was not entitled.*

As Francisco and his entourage sprayed money around Paris like champagne, he came to the attention of an 18-year-old courtesan named Eliza Lynch. After one night of passion with her, he promised to make her the 'Empress of South America'. His Napoleonic dream was to unite South America under the rule of Paraguay, which was the richest country in the region at the time due to the sale of the narcotic yerba maté. Eliza encouraged Francisco's Napoleonic delusions. Eliza, like the Empress Eugenie, was from a humble background, but saw no reason why she should not also – like Eugenie – become an empress.

Francisco and Eliza went on a shopping trip around Europe, dining with the Pope and the notorious Queen Isabella of Spain. When they arrived back in Paraguay, however, although Francisco was treated as a conquering hero, Eliza was snubbed as an 'Irish prostitute'. She was also dismayed by Asunción which was little more than a shanty town – hardly an imperial capital. At her instigation, Francisco built a new customs house, a national library, an arsenal, a railway station with a railway, a new cathedral and an opera – a replica of La Scala in Milan. Unfortunately the architect did not know how to build a roof for the latter and it only got one in 1955. Francisco also built himself a tomb – a replica of Bonaparte's tomb at Les Invalides.

He built up the army, which was soon six times the size of the pre-Civil War US Army, and as his father Carlos lay dying, staged a coup in which he arrested his brother and the two executors of Carlos's will. One of them died from maltreatment; the other – a Catholic priest – was tortured until he made a public statement, printed in the state newspaper, admitting every type of vice, including the ravishing of virtually every woman in the country. When he emerged from jail, he was so changed he went on to become Francisco's chief torturer.

A congress was called to proclaim Francisco president. Those who opposed him were imprisoned, tortured and killed. The congress also granted Francisco a massive pay rise and recognized Eliza as first lady. Francisco's next step was to invade Brazil, followed by an incursion into Argentinian territory.

Argentina and Brazil, although traditional enemies, recognized that Francisco was little better than a mad dog, and soon joined forces with Uruguay in a triple alliance against Paraguay.

López was an international pariah for ignoring the diplomatic niceties and not making a formal declaration of war before attacking. Paraguay was blockaded and soon the Paraguayans were starving. Even so Francisco rejected all peace overtures. Any military setback was viewed as disloyalty and punished with torture and execution, though Francisco himself was terrified of bullets and cowered inside a fortified casement. He also became increasingly paranoid, seeing conspiracies everywhere. As a result he killed more of his own men than the Brazilians and Argentines, who prosecuted the war with extreme caution.

After three years of war, the Brazilian navy forced its way past the Paraguayan fort of Humaitá and Francisco was forced to withdraw. More hastily constructed earth forts were built up the river, but each in turn was overtaken. Asunción was evacuated and the entire population of Paraguay was marched into the interior. Those who could not keep up were killed. Many died of hunger while Francisco, Eliza and their children ate gourmet meals from the best china and swigged champagne from crystal. Periodically, the column would stop for trials when Francisco suspected further conspiracies. Hundreds were slaughtered. Francisco had his two brothers tortured and executed. His two sisters were imprisoned in cages on the back of buffalo carts and his ageing mother regularly flogged until she said that he was her only legitimate son. Francisco also took time off from his retreat to have himself canonized by compliant priests.

On 1 March 1870, the Brazilians, under Princess Isabella's husband the Comte d'Eu, caught up with the retreating column at Cerro Corá in the remote north-east corner of the country. Francisco fled and was caught fording a small stream. When he refused to surrender, he was shot and killed – possibly by a Paraguayan.

More than a million people had died in the war, making it the biggest war in the Americas. Nearly all the male population were wiped out. When the women made their way back to Asunción, they were emaciated and naked, and easy prey for the soldiers garrisoned there and the crooks and chancers who flocked there from all over the globe.

During the war Francisco and, to a greater extent, Eliza had looted the country. She had sent the entire treasure abroad, robbed the womenfolk of their jewels, stole land, pillaged houses and stripped churches. Caught fleeing through the jungle in a ball gown, she was forced to dig the graves of Francisco and her oldest son, who was cut down defending his mother, with her bare hands. But she was a beautiful woman, and the Brazilians took pity on her, smuggling her out of the country. She returned to London, where, despite her vast, stolen riches, she continued suing the Paraguayan and Argentine governments for other goods she claimed they were withholding. Eventually she returned to France, and died in Paris in 1881, where she was buried in Père Lachaise cemetery.

After another disastrous war, this time against Bolivia, in the 1930s, Colonel Rafael Franco seized power in Asunción, making Paraguay Latin America's first Fascist state. Remains – probably not Francisco's – were disinterred from Cerro Corá and brought to Asunción to be laid to rest with all due ceremony in the Panteón de los Héroes, as Francisco's replica of Napoleon's tomb is now named.

In 1961, the new dictator of Paraguay, General Alfredo Stroessner, wanted to do the same with Eliza Lynch. The story goes that a Lebanese drug-dealer seeking to ingratiate himself with the Stroessner regime climbed over the wall of Père Lachaise cemetery one night and dug her up. Again, he probably got the wrong body. He smuggled the remains back to Paraguay in a coffin full of hash. Stroessner declared Eliza a National Heroine and planned to have her laid to rest alongside Francisco in the Panteón de los Héroes. But, at the last moment, the Catholic Church objected as the couple had not been married – even though it was unlikely they would break the seventh commandment again as they had both been dead over 80 years. So the remains were marched in the front door of Panteón de los Héroes and straight out of the back. They gathered dust for nine years in the Museo Lynch – which was little more than a broom cupboard next to the men's lavatory on the first floor of the ministry of defence. Then on 1 March 1970, the hundredth anniversary of Paraguay's defeat in the War of the Triple Alliance, they were interred with due ceremony in the tallest marble mausoleum in South America in the national cemetery at La Recollecta. Huge statues of Francisco and Eliza now dominate Asunción. Paraguay, once the richest country in the region, has never recovered from their attentions.

# Life and Crimes

**1827** Born in Asunción on 24 July.

**1845** Named 'Hero of Corrientes' for futile intervention in Argentine civil war.

**1854** Visits Paris; meets Eliza Lynch; promises to make her 'Empress of South America'.

**1855** Returns to Asunción with Eliza.

**1862** Puts 80,000 men under arms in an army six times the size of that of the pre-Civil War United States.

**1863** Succeeds to power.

**1864** Seizes Brazilian steamer and invades the Matto Grosso.

**1865** Overruns Corrientes and threatens Rio Grande do Sul; on 1 May Brazil, Argentina and Uruguay sign 'Triple Alliance' against Paraguay.

**1866** Paraguayan army falls back to the fort of Humaitá after being defeated on land and on the river.

**1868** Forced to retreat from Humaitá.

**1870** Francisco killed at Cerro Corá.

**1936** Francisco declared National Hero.

**1961** Eliza Lynch declared National Heroine.

# Antonio Guzmán Blanco
## ◄ 1829–1899 ►
## PRESIDENT OF VENEZUELA

After Venezuela won its independence from Spain in 1821, it soon descended into a prolonged period of civil war and was ruled by a series of caudillos, or military dictators. The most powerful of these was Antonio Guzmán Blanco.

He was the son of the famous journalist and politician Leocadio Guzmán, who had married into the wealthy Blanco family. Blanco rose to power on the liberal side in the civil war. He won the support of provincial caudillos and consolidated his position by becoming a special finance commissioner who negotiated loans from London bankers.

In 1870, he seized control of Venezuela as head of the Regeneración movement and three years later had himself elected constitutional president. His rule was anything but liberal. He gagged the press, murdered his political opponents and attacked the church, suppressing religious communities and confiscating their property. He did nothing to help the poor, but made himself rich by skimming profits from the loans he negotiated and his government was riddled with corruption.

However, under his dictatorship public buildings, railroads and schools were built, and Caracas was modernized to function as the centre of the new network of telegraph, ports and roads. He also sponsored public education, restored public credit, subsidised agriculture and promoted international trade. Coffee production increased rapidly.

His government was responsible for the creation of the modern currency – the bolívar – and restored the national anthem 'Gloria al Bravo Pueblo' (Glory to the Brave People). He ordered the body of Simón Bolívar to be exhumed and reburied in the National Pantheon of Venezuela, as if co-opting *El Liberator*'s approval post-mortem, despite the two men's diverging views.

He spent much of his 19-year reign holidaying in Europe, hobnobbing with the aristocracy there. While he was away in Europe in 1889, he was ousted from power by a coup and spent the last years of his life in exile in Paris. He was buried in Passy Cemetery but, after a hundred years, his remains were returned to Venezuela and he lies alongside Bolívar in the National Pantheon. His country house – *La Pequeña Versalles* or Little Versailles – in the region of Antímano was restored in 2004 and has been declared a National Monument.

## Life and Crimes

**1829**　Born 28 February in Caracas, Venezuela.
**1870**　Seizes power.
**1873**　Has himself elected president.
**1889**　Ousted in coup.
**1899**　Dies 20 July in Paris.

# Leopold II
## ◄ 1835–1909 ►
## KING OF BELGIUM

Belgium was only established as a nation in 1831, so it was a late starter in the race to build an empire. However, its second king, Leopold II, was an ambitious man. Like the rest of Europe, he turned his eyes to Africa. He paid Henry Morton Stanley – the rescuer of Dr Livingstone – to explore the Congo. This led to the establishment of the Congo Free State, under the personal sovereignty of Leopold, in 1885. But reports of the atrocities committed in Leopold's name there appalled the world and the Belgian state itself forced Leopold to hand over the Congo in 1908.

The Congo was rich in ivory, but even richer in 'black ivory' – slaves. Although the British had outlawed slavery in 1833 and sent the Royal Navy into the Atlantic to stop the western trade, the trade to the east still flourished. Indeed, the slave trade was only outlawed in the Arabian Peninsula in 1970.

Although Leopold publicly issued anti-slavery edicts, he made Tippu Tip, a slave trader from Zanzibar, governor of the Congo's eastern province, at the same time 'buying' the 'freedom' of several thousand of Tippu Tip's slaves, who were then press-ganged into the Force Publique, the Congo's militia, and used to enslave the rest of the population.

There is an eyewitness account of what it was like to be taken into slavery by Leopold's men. It comes from a woman named Ilanga. She told an American journalist: 'A large band of soldiers came to the village, and ran into the houses and dragged the people out. Three or four came to our house and caught hold of me, my husband Oleka and my sister Katinga. We were all crying, for we knew that we were to be taken away as slaves. The soldiers beat us with the iron sticks from their guns and forced us to march to the camp of Kibalanga. When we were all collected – there were many from other villages we did not know, and many from Waniendo – the soldiers brought baskets of food for us to carry, some of which contained smoked human flesh...

'We then set off marching very quickly. My sister Katinga had her baby in her arms, and was not forced to carry a basket. But my husband Oleka was made to carry a goat. We marched until the afternoon, when we camped near a stream. We were glad to be able to have a drink there because we were very thirsty. But the soldiers gave us nothing to eat… The next day we continued the march, and when we camped at noon were given some maize and plantains, which had been taken from near a deserted village – the people had run away. It continued like this for five days. Then the soldiers took my sister's baby and threw it on the grass, leaving it to die, and made her carry some cooking pots. On the sixth day we became very weak from lack of food and from constant marching and from sleeping on damp grass. My husband, who marched behind with a goat, could not stand up any longer. So he sat down beside the path and refused to walk any more. The soldiers beat him, but still he refused to move. Then one of them struck him on the head with the butt of his rifle and he sprawled on the ground. One of the soldiers caught the goat, while two or three others stuck the long knives they put on the end of their guns into my husband. I saw blood spurt out, and then saw him no more. We had passed over the brow of a hill and he was out of sight. Many of the young men were killed in the same way… After ten days, we came to the great water… and were taken in canoes across to the white men's town at Nyangwe.'

Later, Leopold ordered that children be separated from their parents and organized into three children's colonies where they would be taught Christianity and be trained as soldiers. But the missionaries and the colonies said that they should only take orphans. The Force Publique took this as an excuse to butcher the children's parents then force march the children to the colonies. Thousands perished. Of a column of 108 boys on a forced march to a state colony at Boma in 1892, only 62 made it to their destination, and eight of them died in the next few weeks. The colonies themselves were rife with disease and their mortality rate was 50 per cent. Still, some survived to become soldiers.

In the 1890s, there was a rubber boom – and the Congo was full of wild rubber, which came from vines, rather than trees. However, it would need vast manpower to harvest and brutal methods were adopted. According to the British vice consul: 'The Force Publique would arrive in canoes at a village, the inhabitants of which invariably bolted on their arrival. The soldiers were then landed, and commenced looting, taking all the chickens, grain, etc., out of the houses. After this they attacked the natives until able to seize their women. These women were kept as hostages until the chief of the district brought the required number of kilograms of rubber. The rubber having been brought, the women were sold back to their owners for a couple of goats apiece, and so [they] continued from village to village.'

The wife of any man refusing to collect rubber would be killed. She might die anyway as the conditions were harsh and food scarce in the stockades where they were held. The soldiers guarding the women would also take the prettiest and rape them.

This method of collecting rubber was recommended by the official manuals handed out in Africa. Once the system got going, every village was assigned a quota. This was usually three to four kilos of dried rubber per adult male per fortnight. Hundreds of thousands of men were conscripted this way. They were overseen by the Force Publique who built garrisons throughout the rubber-growing areas. Men had to carry their heavy load of rubber for miles to deliver it to the company agents. They would get paid in trinkets or a few spoonfuls of salt. One chief was paid in people. He was told he could eat them, kill them, or use them as slaves – anything he liked.

*King Leopold II's tyranny was focused on the Congo, where he established his own private state and headed a deadly and exploitative regime.*

When a village resisted, the Force Publique would be employed to terrorize them. Ten hostages would be taken, tied up in a tent with large stones and pushed into a river. The women would then be raped. Sometimes the Force Publique would simply shoot everyone to intimidate other villages. But for every bullet they were issued, the soldiers would have to return one right hand. Sometimes, more drastic methods were employed.

'One example was enough,' said Belgian officer Léon Fiévez in 1894. 'A hundred heads were cut off, and there have been plenty of supplies around the station ever since... My goal is ultimately humanitarian. I killed 100 people, but allowed 500 others to live.'

Leopold wanted to open the country up with a railway. Of the 540 Chinese construction workers brought in from Hong Kong and Macao in 1892, 300 died on the job or ran away into the forests. Several hundred workers came in from Barbados. When they realized they were in the Congo, they rioted. The soldiers opened fire on them. The survivors were taken to the railhead and put to work. Tropical diseases, lack of food, no shelter, relentless floggings, engines that ran off the track and boxcars full of dynamite that exploded cost the lives of nearly 2,000 men in the eight-year construction of the first stretch of track.

News of what was happening in the Congo began to get out. In 1897, a Swedish Baptist missionary told a meeting in London that Force Publique soldiers were rewarded for the number of hands they brought in. A soldier had told him: 'The Commissioner has promised us if we have plenty of hands he will shorten our service. I have brought in plenty of hands already, and I expect my time of service will soon be finished.'

The British press were already gunning for Leopold. In 1895, a Belgian officer had 'dared to kill an Englishman' – actually the victim was an Irishman who had 'gone native' and married an African woman. When his ivory business challenged Leopold's monopoly, the Force Publique was sent. They hanged the Irishman, and London's press howled in outrage.

Leopold countered the bad press he was getting by creating the Commission for the Protection of the Natives, comprising six Belgian Catholics and six foreign missionaries. But he cleverly picked commissioners who lived so far apart that the commission only met twice and then only three attended.

The world's fair took place in Brussels in 1897. The Belgian exhibit included 267 Africans brought from the Congo, living happily in an African village set up for them in a park in Brussels. Ninety of them were members of the Force Publique. At a gala dinner, a black sergeant proposed a toast to King Leopold.

In the scramble to fulfil quotas the rubber vines were killed off. The Budja tribe rebelled, killing 30 soldiers, then fled. A punitive expedition was sent against them, led by an American rubber agent named Edgar Canisius.

'As our party moved through village after village, a party of men had been detailed with torches to fire every hut,' he wrote. 'As we progressed, a line of smoke hung over the jungle for many miles, announcing to the natives far and wide that civilization was dawning... The porters had an especially hard time, for many of them were chained together by the neck. They carried our boxes slung on poles, and when one fell down he usually brought down all his companions on the same chain. Many of the poor wretches became so exhausted by this kind of marching that they could be urged forward only by blows from rifles. Some had their shoulders so chafed by the poles that they literally shrieked with pain.'

By the time Canisius caught up with the Budjas, the porters were done for and his prisoners had to take over. 'All were compelled to carry heavy loads, each of which required two men to transport... until they finally succumbed to starvation and smallpox.'

Roger Casement, the Irish nationalist later executed for treason, was then working for the Foreign Office. He was sent to the Congo as consul and reported back the brutalities he had witnessed. He discovered that soldiers did not just cut off the hands of their victims. When accused of killing only women, they castrated their victims to prove otherwise.

Casement's reports provoked a debate in Parliament. Newspapers across Europe began reporting the atrocities in the Congo. Stories emerged of mass murder, where entire villages and towns had been wiped out, brutal beatings, mutilations, rapes, mass starvation and epidemics of smallpox and other diseases the whites had brought. In all, 10 million people died as a result of Leopold's tyrannical reign.

His response was to stage show trials of particularly brutal Belgian rubber agents. Their defence was that the natives were lazy and terror tactics were necessary to make them work. Most were acquitted and those found guilty escaped with light sentences.

The King of the Belgians seemed to be riding out the storm. But then the 65-year-old Leopold took up with a 16-year-old prostitute. This turned his people against him and made him a ridiculous figure in the eyes of the world, especially when he took her with him to Queen Victoria's funeral in 1901.

Social reformer Edmund Morel set up the Congo Reform Association with branches throughout Britain, and every Sunday members would be regaled with reports of atrocities from eye witnesses. This one came from a missionary, the Reverend John Harris:

'Lined up were 40 emaciated sons of an African village, each carrying his little basket of rubber. The toll of rubber is weighed and accepted, but four baskets were short of the demand. The order is brutally short and sharp. Quickly the first defaulter is seized by four lusty executioners, thrown on the bare ground, pinioned hands and feet, whilst a fifth steps forward carrying a long whip of twisted hippo hide. Swiftly and without cessation the whip falls, and the sharp corrugated edges cut deep into the flesh – on back, shoulders and buttocks blood spurts from a dozen places. In vain the victim twists in the grip of the executioners, and then the whip cuts other parts of the quivering body – and in the case of one of the four, upon the most sensitive parts of the human frame. The 100 lashes each left four inert bodies bloody and quivering on the sand of the rubber collecting point.'

Morel took his campaign to America, where Leopold paid lobbyists in Washington to defend his case. When one of these lobbyists was discovered trying to bribe members of Congress, however, atrocities in the Congo began to make the front pages.

To try and stem the tide of criticism, Leopold set up a new Commission of Enquiry with three judges – one Belgian, one Swiss, one Italian. Again he picked shrewdly. The judges knew no African languages, nor did they speak enough English to talk to the highly critical British and American missionaries who were leading the international campaign. More, the Italian, Giacomo Nisco, had been chief judge in the Congo. He was convinced of the need for stern discipline and had let Belgian officers found guilty of atrocities off with light sentences.

Nevertheless, the evidence they collected was so overwhelming it could not be ignored. They collected 370 depositions. One came from Chief Lontulu of Bolima, who had been flogged, held hostage and set to work in chains. He laid on the table of the commission 110 twigs, one for each member of his tribe who had been murdered in the quest for rubber. He divided the twigs into four piles – one for tribal nobles, one for men, one for women and one for children. Then he put a name to each of the twigs.

The testimony of Chief Lontulu and the other witnesses was so damning that the governor-general, the man nominally responsible for the system slit his own throat. During the account of one atrocity one of the judges broke down and wept.

The commissioners returned to Europe and wrote their report. It was damning. But Leopold still had one trick up his sleeve. The day before the report was published, every major newspaper in England received a document purporting to be a 'complete and authentic résumé of the report'. It came from the West African Missionary Association. The newspapers were delighted. Not only did it give them a one-day jump on the big story of the week, it was in English. Associated Press sent it on to America.

When the report itself came out, however, the papers realized that the summary was nowhere near as damning as the report itself. Worse, the West African Missionary Association did not actually exist: the 'summary' had been delivered by a Belgian priest whose church had recently received a large donation by Leopold.

The full report detailed one atrocity after another – fatal beatings, random killings, senseless acts of cruelty. One woman who was making bricks had clay forced into her vagina by the overseer. All the Belgian agent said was: 'If you die working for me, they'll throw you in the river.' And there was page after page after page on the severing of hands.

One man reported that, when he and a companion had been on their way to testify, they had been seized by a Belgian officer and hung from a tree for several days. Then they were beaten around the neck and private parts with a stick. His companion died and his body was thrown in the river.

The British and American governments began to put pressure on the Belgian government, but they did not control the Congo: it was Leopold's personal possession. When the Belgian government tried to buy it from him, and government auditors examined the books, they discovered that 32 million francs the government had lent Leopold were missing. They suspected he had given the money to his teenage mistress. The money was written off along with 110 million francs' worth of debt, much of it in the form of bonds given to Leopold's teenage mistress and the king's other lovers. And Leopold received another 100 million francs in compensation. But his atrocity-studded rule in the Congo was over. The Congo became part of Belgium in 1908. Leopold died the following year.

## Life and Crimes

**1835** Born 9 April in Brussels.

**1865** Succeeds his father, Leopold I, to the Belgian throne.

**1876** Backs Sir Henry Morton Stanley's expedition to explore the Congo.

**1885** Gains US recognition of his personal sovereignty over the Congo Free State.

**1892** Rebellion of railway workers put down by gunfire; 54 boys die on death march.

**1895** British press in uproar when one Irish subject killed by Belgians.

**1897** Swedish missionary tells meeting in London that soldiers were rewarded for collecting severed hands.

**1899** British vice consul reports on brutality of the rubber trade in the Congo.

**1901** Leopold takes 16-year-old prostitute with him to Queen Victoria's funeral.

**1904** Investigation exposes the full horrors of the rubber trade in the Congo.

**1908** Leopold forced to sell the Congo to the Belgian state.

**1909** Dies 17 December in Belgium.

# Mwanga II
### ◄ 1868–1903 ►
## KABAKA OF BUGANDA

When Mutesa I of Buganda – modern-day Uganda – died in 1884, he was succeeded by his son Mwanga, the first Ugandan Kabaka to take the throne without executing anyone. This promising beginning was short-lived. While Mutesa had been erratic and two faced, Mwanga was brutal, sadistic, and paranoid, though crafty, with flashes of keen intelligence. Although initially in favour of the Christians his father had encouraged, once he realized that their primary loyalty was to their God and not to him, he made an abrupt volte-face, and by the end of the first year of his reign, had roasted three Christians alive. Late in 1885 Mwanga had a visiting bishop assassinated at the border of his lands, perceiving the bishop to be a threat to his rule.

At this point Mwanga's madness and paranoia led him to become totally unhinged. He turned on the Christian communities, both Catholic and Protestant. Part of his rage was brought to a head by the fact that many of his court pages had embraced the new faith, and as a result were resisting his amorous advances towards them. These young men became a special focus for his wrath, which soon became a full-blown persecution.

The witch hunt was carried out with an efficiency matched only by the courage of the victims. One eyewitness description of the arrest, trial and execution of a man named Munyaga reads as follows: 'Munyaga begged to be allowed to put on his kansu (white gown worn by Bugandan Christians), which they agreed to, and then they led him away. After a cruel mockery of a trial, he was ordered to be hacked in pieces and burned. His torturers cut off one of his arms and flung it into the fire before him, then they cut off a leg, and that too, was flung into the flame, and lastly, the poor mutilated body was laid on the framework to be consumed'. On the same day, 32 other converts were roasted over a slow fire.

When the executioner reported to Mwanga after the executions, and marvelled that all the victims had gone to their deaths calling on God,

Mwanga shrugged his shoulders and remarked that God could not have been paying much attention.

For nearly a year as Mwanga continued to bugger his unconverted pages while out of his mind on hemp and rotgut home-fermented spirit, more than 200 Christians were hacked to pieces and burnt alive. It was, as another eyewitness put it, 'a martyrdom as terrible as any in Christian history'.

Mwanga's violent dementia would prove to be his downfall.

When the rumour went around that all Christians and Muslims would be rounded up and executed, members of both faiths stormed Mwanga's palace and deposed him. Although Mwanga regained his throne, the British kept a careful watch over him, and finally deposed him, and exiled him to the Seychelles in 1899, where he died four years later.

# Life and Crimes

**1868** Born H.H. Danieri Basamula-Ekkeri Mwanga II Mukasa.

**1885** Has three Christians burnt alive.

**1885** Orders the murder of a visiting bishop.

**1886** Begins persecution of Christians on a grand scale.

**1888** Deposed by combined Muslim and Christian rebels.

**1889** Regains throne.

**1899** Exiled by the British to the Seychelles.

**1903** Dies.

# THE MODERN WORLD

The 20th century was dominated by global wars. World War I resulted in a new breed of tyrant. It spawned Fascist dictators in Germany, Italy and Spain, while in Russia Lenin established what was called 'the dictatorship of the proletariat'. The result was summary execution, bulging prisons and labour camps. Both systems extinguished individual freedom in favour of the state. World War II left a handful of tyrants in Eastern Europe, while the post-war decolonization of Africa left newly independent countries without the political or legal infrastructure to prevent tyrants from taking over. Meanwhile, in Latin America there was a fresh crop of *caudillos*.

# Porfirio Díaz

## ◄ 1830–1915 ►

## DICTATOR OF MEXICO

Like many tyrants, Porfirio Díaz came to power on the back of a democratic revolution, only to turn into a repressive dictator.

Born to a humble *mestizo* family in Mexico in 1830, Díaz studied to become a priest, but he abandoned the seminary to join the army at the outbreak of the war with the United States in 1846. He went on to distinguish himself in the War of the Reform – a civil war – from 1857 to 1860, and in 1861, he was elected the federal representative from the state of Oaxaca.

In the struggle against the French between 1861 and 1867, he backed the liberals under Benito Juárez. His contribution was key to the collapse

*President Diaz, ex-soldier of the revolution and dictator of Mexico.*

of the French-backed regime, which installed the Emperor Maximilian, and the establishment of a republic under Juárez. But when Juárez stood for re-election in 1871, Díaz led a rebellion which failed. However, he defeated Juárez's hand-picked successor Sebastian Lerdo de Tejada in the election of 1876. Falling from power in 1880, Díaz was re-elected in 1884 and held power until 1911.

Díaz believed in economic growth at any price. This meant marginalizing the poor and expropriating the land of the Indians, who made up two-thirds of the population. The result was the rise of groups of bandits, who would later become a guerrilla force under Pancho Villa. To combat them, Díaz established the powerful state police force called the *rurales*. But rather than chase bandits, they preferred to terrorize Indian communities.

Díaz's economic miracle did not work. In 1910, the aristocratic but democratically minded reformer Francisco Madero ran against him. When Díaz fixed the election, Madero organized a military coup. Díaz resigned on 25 May 1911 and went into exile in France, where he died on 2 July 1915.

## Life and Crimes

**1830** Born 15 September in Oaxaca.

**1846** Joins the army to fight the United States.

**1857–1860** Distinguishes himself in the War of the Reform.

**1861–1867** Helps overthrow the French-backed regime in Mexico.

**1871** Stages abortive coup against Benito Juárez.

**1876** Elected president.

**1884–1910** Dispossesses the poor and terrorizes Indian communities.

**1910** Fixes election.

**1911** Overthrown by Francisco Madero in military coup.

**1915** Dies 2 July in exile in Paris.

# Tzu-hsi

◄ 1835–1908 ►

## DOWAGER EMPRESS OF CHINA

Although Tzu-hsi started as a lowly concubine, she ended up ruling China for over 50 years, after her great beauty brought her to the attention of the Emperor Hsien-feng, and she bore his only son Tung-chih. When Hsien-feng died, Tung-chih was only 6 years old, so Tzu-hsi ruled as regent, brutally suppressing the Taiping Rebellion in 1864 and the Nien Rebellion in 1868.

When Tung-chih came of age in 1873, Tzu-hsi refused to relinquish power. Two years later, he died – some say at his mother's hand. In violation of all the laws of succession, Tzu-hsi placed Tung-chih's three-year-old cousin Kuang-hsü on the throne, with herself, once again, as regent. Although her full title was 'Mother Auspicious Orthodox Heaven-Blessed Prosperous All-Nourishing Brightly-Manifest Calm

*The funeral procession of the Empress Dowager of China, Empress Tzu-hsi.*

Sedate Perfect Long-Lived Respectful Reverend Worshipful Illustrious Exalted Empress Dowager', she was known in the Forbidden City as 'The Old Buddha'.

When Kuang-hsü came of age in 1889, Tzu-hsi retired to a summer palace she had built with the money set aside to modernize the Chinese navy. But when Kuang-hsü began instituting radical reforms, Tzu-hsi staged a coup and had the emperor imprisoned in his palace, while she ruled in his stead.

In 1900, she encouraged the Boxer Rebellion which aimed to drive out all foreigners from China. When this was brutally put down by European troops, she fled Beijing and was eventually forced to sign a humiliating peace treaty in 1902.

The day before Tzu-hsi died on 15 November 1908, Kuang-hsü was killed in accordance with her deathbed wishes.

## Life and Crimes

**1835** Born in obscurity.

**1861** Becomes regent of China.

**1875** Son dies in suspicious circumstances; continues as regent for three-year-old cousin.

**1889** Retires to summer palace.

**1895** Imprisons emperor and seizes power again.

**1900** Encourages Boxer Rebellion: forced to flee when this fails.

**1908** Dies 15 November after ordering murder of the emperor.

# Vladimir Ilyich Lenin
## ◀ 1870–1924 ▶
## LEADER OF THE USSR

Born Vladimir Ilyich Ulyanov to a prosperous middle-class family, he adopted the pseudonym Lenin in 1901 after being exiled to Siberia for revolutionary activities after his beloved elder brother was hanged for plotting against the tsar.

Working as a party organizer, journalist and pamphleteer, Lenin spent much of his life abroad, founding his revolutionary Bolshevik Party during his exile in London where he lived for nine years. This would push, not for the equality of the masses, but for the dictatorship of a revolutionary elite – some feared, of one man.

A democratic revolution had already taken place against the tsar in Russia when in 1917 the Germans allowed Lenin to return from exile in Switzerland, crossing enemy territory in a 'closed train', in the hope that he would take Russia permanently out of World War I. He called for armed insurrection and in the first week of November – October in the 'Old Style' Julian calendar – he staged the October Revolution, overthrowing the moderate provisional government.

He rejected all calls to enter into a coalition with other socialist parties and his Communist Party organization quickly seized control of every aspect of Russian life, while his secret police, the Cheka, sought out class enemies for mass execution. 'How can you make a revolution without firing squads?' he said.

He signed a peace treaty with the Central Powers, pulling out of World War I and instituted the Red Terror. Tens of thousands were killed or interned in labour camps. Religion was suppressed and the press censored. Baltic states and countries in eastern Europe that were formerly part of the Russian Empire were taken over by the Communists and the Comintern was set up to export Communism worldwide.

In July 1918, Tsar Nicholas Romanov II and his entire family were shot in Siberia. Lenin fought a bitter civil war against the anti-Communist forces,

*Lenin addresses a revolutionary crowd of soldiers and sailors, Moscow, 1918.*

emerging victorious in 1921. He then forced through the collectivization of farming, causing a famine which killed six million.

While Lenin was in London, the British knew that he was a dangerous revolutionary, but when he went back to Russia they sent agents to assassinate him in an effort to prevent Russia making peace on the Eastern Front. He was shot, twice, and it was feared that he was going to die. The British Embassy in St Petersburg was invaded and the British military attaché killed, and the British consul in Moscow was arrested.

A surgeon was flown in from Berlin who removed a bullet from his lung, but left the second bullet in his neck. Slowly his health began to decline due to lead poisoning. He died in 1924, making way for an even more bloodthirsty tyrant – Josef Stalin.

# Life and Crimes

**1870** Born 22 April in Simbirsk, later renamed Ulyanov after him.

**1887** Elder brother hanged for plotting against the tsar; begins reading Marx.

**1891** Graduates as a lawyer from the University of St Petersburg.

**1893** Becomes full-time revolutionary.

**1895** Exiled to Siberia.

**1903** Founds the Bolshevik party.

**1917** Returns to Russia in closed train; seizes power; signs armistice with Germany; begins civil war.

**1918** Shot by would-be assassin; orders the execution of the tsar and his family.

**1919** Founds Comintern to export revolution.

**1921** Wins civil war.

**1921–1923** Famine caused by collectivization of farming wipes out six million.

**1924** Dies of stroke 21 January in Gorki near Moscow.

# The Three Pashas

◄ 1872–1922 ►

## RULERS OF THE OTTOMAN EMPIRE

From the 14th century, the Ottoman or Turkish Empire extended across much of Southeast Europe, West Asia and North Africa. But by 1913, it had been driven out of most of Europe and North Africa, leaving the government in Constantinople, later Istanbul, in control of Turkey, Syria, Iraq, Lebanon, Palestine, Transjordan and the Red Sea coast of the Arabian peninsula.

That year, there was a coup d'état where the pro-British government was overthrown by the Committee of Union and Progress, the leading faction of the Young Turk movement that had ended the absolute power of the Sultan in 1908. In 1913, a triumvirate of CUP leader Mehmed Talât, Ismail Enver and Ahmed Cemal, took control. They adopted the honorific Pasha, ruling as Talât Pasha, Enver Pasha and Cemal Pasha – the Three Pashas.

Talât Pasha was Grand Vizier, or prime minister, and Minister of the Interior. Enver Pasha was Minister of War and Cemal Pasha was Minister of the Navy. Theirs was an authoritarian rule with Talât Pasha gradually eclipsing the others. They brought Turkey into World War I on the side of Germany.

On the orders of Talât Pasha, an estimated 1 to 1.5 million Armenians were sent on death marches to the Syrian Desert in 1915 and 1916 because of their supposed allegiance to Russia and their Christian faith. The deportees were deprived of food and water and subjected to robbery, rape and massacres. In the Syrian Desert, the survivors were kept in concentration camps. In 1916, another wave of massacres was ordered, leaving about 200,000 deportees alive by the end of the year. Around 100,000 to 200,000 Armenian women and children were forcibly converted to Islam and integrated into Muslim households. Some 300,000 Assyrians and 750,000 Greeks also perished.

Defeat in World War I left Turkey stripped of its possessions in the Middle East beyond its current borders. The Three Pashas fled and were sentenced to death *in absentia* by a military tribunal. Talât and Cemal were assassinated. Enver died fighting in a Muslim revolt against the Bolsheviks in Central Asia.

# Lives and Crimes

**1872**  Ahmed Cemal born 6 May.

**1874**  Mehmed Talât born 1 September.

**1881**  Ismail Enver born 22 November.

**1893**  Cemal joins the army.

**1896**  Talât jailed again for membership of the CUP.

**1898**  Cemal joins the CUP; Talât exiled to Salonika (Thessaloniki) as postal clerk.

**1903**  Enver joins fight against Greek, Bulgarian and Serb guerrillas in Macedonia.

**1908**  Talât organizes assassinations during Young Turk Revolution, elected to parliament for the CUP; Enver joins forces with revolutionary hero Ahmed Niyazi.

**1909**  Talât appointed Minister of the Interior, acknowledged head of the CUP and the Young Turks; Enver becomes military attaché in Berlin.

**1911**  Cemal appointed governor of Baghdad; Enver commands troops in Libya in Italo-Turkish War.

**1912**  Cemal fights in the First Balkan War; Talât goes into hiding; Salonika falls to Greece, headquarters of the CUP moves to Constantinople; Enver recalled to Constantinople.

**1913**  Talât, Enver and Cemal seize power.

**1915**  Cemal appointed Governor of Syria; commands two failed attacks on the Suez Canal; Talât closes Armenian political organizations, leaders arrested, murders of Armenians begin; Enver initiates Armenian deportations and massacres.

**1916** Cemal known as 'The Butcher' for hanging Arab nationalist; negotiates the surrender of the British at Kut; Talât orders mass deportation of Armenians, begins Turkification and deportation of the Kurds.

**1917** Cemal oversees the Jaffa deportation where Jews are robbed and killed; Talât becomes Grand Vizier.

**1918** Cemal oversees the Tafas massacre, flees to Switzerland; Talât and Enver seek asylum in Germany.

**1919** Cemal, Talât and Enver stripped of title of Pasha and condemned to death, Enver acts as secret envoy between Berlin and Moscow.

**1921** Talât assassinated in Berlin by Armenian genocide survivor; Enver sent by Lenin to suppress anti-Bolshevik revolt in Central Asia, but switches sides and commands rebel forces.

**1922** Cemal assassinated in Tiflis (Tbilis, Georgia) by Armenians for his part in the genocide; Enver killed in skirmish with Red Army in Tajikistan.

# Syngman Rhee
◀ 1875–1965 ▶
## PRESIDENT OF KOREA

During the Japanese occupation of Korea from 1910 to 1945, Syngman Rhee was in the United States, agitating for Korean independence. In 1919 he was elected president of the Korean Provisional Government in exile.

Returning to Seoul in 1945, he organized strong-arm squads to murder or intimidate political rivals. When talks between the US and the Soviet Union on reunifying the northern and southern zones that they occupied failed in 1948, he stood as president of South Korea. When Kim Il-Sung invaded in 1950, he called for – and received – United Nations' help. However, when the UN tried to make peace, Rhee prolonged the fighting in the hope of total victory. At a crucial moment, he released anti-Communist prisoners of war, infuriating Kim Il-Sung and restarting the war.

Rhee was re-elected in 1952, 1956 and 1960 – with 90 per cent of the vote that year. As president he took dictatorial powers, purging the National Assembly, banning the opposition Progressive Party, and executing its leader for treason. He also controlled the appointment of village mayors and police chiefs.

The blatant election fraud of 1960 provoked student demonstrations, which were suppressed with heavy casualties, but a unanimous vote of the National Assembly called for Rhee's resignation. On 27 April 1960, Rhee went into exile in Hawaii, where he died.

## Life and Crimes

**1875** Born 26 March in Whanghae, Korea.

**1919** Becomes president of the Korean Provisional Government in exile.

**1945** Returns to Korea and eliminates rivals.

**1948** Elected president.

1950   Korean war begins.
1952   Re-elected president.
1953   Scuppers peace talks.
1956   Re-elected with 55 per cent of the vote.
1960   Re-elected with 90 per cent of the vote; students demonstrate; National Assembly demands resignation; flees country.
1965   Dies 19 July, Honolulu, Hawaii.

# Juan Perón
◄ 1895–1974 ►

## PRESIDENT OF ARGENTINA

A career soldier, Juan Perón was Argentina's military attaché to Mussolini's Italy in the 1930s, where he got a master class in how to run a Fascist state.

Returning to Argentina in 1941, he joined a plot which ousted the civilian government in 1943. He became secretary of labour and social welfare in the new military administration, giving him the opportunity to win the support of the *descamisados* – the 'shirtless ones'. He went on to become minister of war and vice-president.

In October 1945, another coup sought to oust the military government and Perón was arrested. But his beautiful mistress, the popular actress Eva Duarte, rallied the workers of Buenos Aires to demand his release. Freed, he made a speech to 300,000 people from the balcony of the presidential palace, promising peace, prosperity and social justice. A few days later, he married Eva – or Evita as she was known.

In February 1946, he was elected president. His popular appeal to the masses was augmented by the use of Fascist-style thugs to intimidate the opposition. Argentina had built up a large foreign-currency surplus from its exports to both sides during World War II and this money was used to fund development projects and benefits for the workers.

Politically, the regime was oppressive. In 1948, enemies including two priests were charged with plotting to assassinate Perón. When a judge refused to accept the government's flagrantly fraudulent evidence, he was removed from the bench. And Evita was reputed to keep a glass jar on her desk filled with the severed genitals of political opponents.

Perón won a second election in 1951 with an increased majority. But Evita died of cancer the following year, plunging the country into mourning. Soon the money was running out and Perón's regime was engulfed by inflation and demagoguery. A coup ousted him in 1955 after it was revealed that, while petitioning the pope to beatify Evita, he was defiling her memory with a 14-year-old mistress.

In exile in Spain he managed to hold on to control of the Perónist movement by encouraging rivalry between competing factions. He married Isabel Martínez, an Argentine dancer, and the couple returned to Argentina in 1973 when elections were called. Perón won the presidency and insisted that his unpopular wife was named vice-president.

With the help of the army, he resumed his terror tactics, driving left-wingers to take up arms in a guerrilla war. Inflation soared once more. Perón died on 1 July 1974 and on 24 March 1976 his wife, who had succeeded him, was ousted. However Perónism has remained a staple in Argentine life, along with corruption and inflation.

## Life and Crimes

**1895** Born 8 October in Buenos Aires province, Argentina.

**1911** Enrols in military school.

**1938** Goes to Italy as military attaché.

**1941** Returns to Argentina.

**1943** Joins plot to oust civilian government.

**1945** Military government overthrown; Perón arrested; Evita organizes rally to set him free; they marry.

**1946** Elected president.

**1951** Re-elected.

**1952** Evita dies.

**1955** Perón ousted; goes into exile in Spain.

**1973** Returns to be elected president.

**1974** Dies 1 July in Buenos Aires.

**1976** Third wife Isabel ousted.

# Josef Stalin
## ◀ 1879–1953 ▶
## LEADER OF THE USSR

Born Josef Vissarionovich Dzhugashvili in Georgia, Stalin did not start to learn Russian until he went to school at the age of eight. He was beaten savagely by his drunken father who died when young Josef was 11, then his doting mother groomed him for the Orthodox priesthood.

At his seminary, he earned the nickname Koba, after a famous Georgian bandit and rebel, for his anti-tsarist views. He quit to become a revolutionary organizer.

When the Social Democrats split in 1903, Koba joined the Bolshevik faction under Lenin. He organized bank robberies to fund the party, joining the Central Committee in 1912, and took the name Stalin, which means 'man of steel'. He became the editor of the Bolshevik paper Pravda – 'Truth' – but was exiled to Siberia in 1913, returning to Petrograd to play a key role in the Communist coup d'état in 1917.

When Lenin died in 1924, Stalin took over, ruthlessly crushing all opposition. In 1928, Stalin began an ambitious Five Year Plan to industrialize Russia, funded by the export of grain, and continued the collectivization of farming which resulted in famine, most notably in the Ukraine. Those who resisted in any way were executed, and a peasants' revolt was savagely put down. It is estimated that 25 million people perished as a result of collectivization.

In 1934, Stalin organized the murder of his colleague and potential rival Sergey Kirov, and then used the assassination as a pretext for a purge. Between 1936 and 1938, there was a series of show trials, with thousands of party officials and senior army officers found guilty of treason and executed. By 1939, of the 1,966 delegates to the 1934 party congress that had backed Kirov, 1,108 were dead; of the 139 members elected to the Central Committee that year, 98 were dead. Meanwhile Stalin's secret police chief Lavrenti Beria, a fellow Georgian, had arrested millions of ordinary people, executing, exiling or imprisoning them in labour camps.

By 1939, there was no opposition in the Soviet Union, but the nation

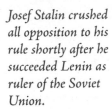

*Josef Stalin crushed all opposition to his rule shortly after he succeeded Lenin as ruler of the Soviet Union.*

had been weakened by the extensive purges. Appalled, the Western nations refused to make any treaties with Stalin, leading him instead to sign a non-aggression pact with Hitler – even though the two were, at least in theory, sworn ideological enemies. Under a secret protocol, they divided Poland between them and Stalin invaded Finland, while Hilter took France and the Low Countries.

But the non-aggression pact was a trick. Once Hitler felt secure in the West, he abrogated the agreement and on 22 June 1941, without warning, invaded the Soviet Union. The Red Army, purged of senior officers, could do little to resist. Thinking all was lost, Stalin was on the point of fleeing Moscow when, at the last minute, he changed his mind.

He took personal control of the army, appointing two brilliant commanders, Georgi Zhukov and Ivan Konev. With no regard for human life, Stalin threw millions of ill-equipped and poorly-trained men into the fight, eventually turning the tide with sheer weight of numbers. Zhukov and Konev slowly and painfully fought their way through to Berlin and victory. Zhukov was rewarded with a distant posting in the east, while Konev remained abroad as commissar for Austria: nothing was to detract from Stalin's image as the hero who had won what the Soviets called 'The Great Patriotic War'.

Stalin forced repressive Communist regimes on the countries of eastern Europe and the Balkans which the Red Army had 'liberated'. Europe was divided in two by, in Winston Churchill's phrase, an 'Iron Curtain' and hostility between East and West would develop into the Cold War.

In 1953, Stalin announced that he had discovered another plot among the – mostly Jewish – doctors in the Kremlin. He seemed ready to begin a new round of purges when, on 5 March 1953, he died of a brain haemorrhage.

# Life and Crimes

**1879** Born 21 December in Gori, Georgia.

**1893** Attends seminary.

**1898** Begins anti-tsarist activities.

**1899** Leaves seminary to become political organizer.

**1903** Joins Bolsheviks.

**1913–1917** Exile in Siberia.

**1917** Plays prominent part in October Revolution.

**1924** Succeeds Lenin.

**1928–1934** Forced collectivization kills 25 million.

**1934** Murders Sergey Kirov.

**1936–1938** Purges party officials and army officers in show trials; secret police murder and imprison millions more.

**1939** Signs pact with Hitler; takes half of Poland; invades Finland.

**1941** Hitler attacks; Stalin prepares to flee; changes his mind at the last minute.

**1941–1945** Pours millions of men into the fight against the invading Germans.

**1945** Claims sole credit for victory over Hitler; imprisons returning prisoners of war.

**1946** Divides Europe with 'Iron Curtain'; begins forcing repressive Communist regimes on Soviet hegemony.

**1953** Uncovers 'doctors' plot'; plans new purge, but dies suddenly on 5 March, before any purge can be implemented.

# Benito Mussolini
## ◄ 1883–1945 ►
### DICTATOR OF ITALY

Teacher-turned-socialist journalist, Benito Mussolini was wounded in the buttocks during World War I, when Italy fought against Germany on the side of the Allies.

Having been expelled from the Socialist party for his support for the war, Mussolini started his own party called the *Fasci di Combattimento* – the 'fasci' evoking the fascae, the bundle of rods with an axe-head protruding that was the symbol of authority in ancient Rome, and 'combattimento' meaning struggle. Although this party was pro-labour and anti-Church, it was also fanatically nationalistic and sought to recreate the power of Italy in the days of the Roman Empire. Backed by industrialists and army officers, Mussolini organized teams of uniformed 'Blackshirts' who fought other political parties on the streets.

On 28 October 1922, the Blackshirts marched on Rome. The government fell and Mussolini was given dictatorial powers by King Victor Emmanuel. He replaced the king's guard with his own fascisti, packed parliament with his own men and set up a secret police force called the Ovra.

Although he famously got the trains to run on time and boosted industrial production by cutting taxes, he turned against labour, brutally repressing strikes. He seized Corfu from Greece and the port of Fiume, or Rijeka, from Yugoslavia.

In 1924 he held elections, the result of which had already been fixed. When the Socialist leader Giacomo Matteotti spoke out, he was found murdered. Mussolini responded to the resulting crisis by making Italy a one-party state with himself as 'Il Duce' – 'The Leader'. Other political opponents were killed, trade unions were banned and an accommodation was made with the Catholic Church.

Dreaming of a new Roman Empire, Mussolini invaded Abyssinia – modern Ethiopia – in 1935, gassing and bombing its defenceless inhabitants, and annexing the country in 1936 despite the condemnation of the – frankly toothless – League of Nations, the forerunner of the United Nations. He entered the 'Pact of Steel' with Hitler and gave military support to Franco in Spain.

In April 1939, Mussolini invaded Albania and in June 1940 joined World War II on Germany's side by attacking France. However, his military disasters in Greece and Libya forced Hitler to commit badly needed troops to the Balkans and North Africa.

After Sicily fell to the Allies in July 1943, Mussolini was dismissed and arrested, and Italy changed sides. Imprisoned on 12 September, Mussolini was rescued by a daring German commando raid, led by Hitler's super soldier, *SS-Sturmbannführer* Otto Skorzeny. With Hitler's backing he set up a new Fascist state in northern Italy, which was still under German occupation, and executed those who he felt had betrayed him – including his son-in-law Count Galeazzo Ciano.

The Allied drive up the Italian peninsula, however, was unstoppable, and, true to form, in April 1945 Mussolini and his mistress Clara Petacci fled. Captured by Italian partisans on the Austrian border, they were executed by firing squad and their bodies were hung upside down in the Piazza Loreto in Milan.

*Mussolini parades through the streets of Florence, May 1938, during a state visit from fellow dictator Adolf Hitler.*

# Life and Crimes

**1883**  Born 29 July in Predappio, Italy.

**1912**  Becomes editor of socialist newspaper Avanti!

**1914**  Starts pro-war newspaper Il Popolo d'Italia; expelled from Socialist party.

**1915**  Joins Italian army as private.

**1917**  Wounded in the buttocks.

**1918**  Advocates the emergence of a dictator; hints that he might be the man.

**1919**  Begins the Fascist party Fasci di Combattimento.

**1922**  Marches on Rome; becomes Italy's youngest prime minister with dictatorial powers; seizes Corfu and Rijeka.

**1924**  Secures power with fraudulent election; murders opponents.

**1929**  Signs Lateran Treaty, guaranteeing pope's sovereignty in Vatican.

**1935**  Invades Abyssinia, gassing and bombing the populace.

**1936**  Annexes Abyssinia, announcing new Roman Empire; signs Pact of Steel with Hitler; sends troops to fight for Franco in Spain.

**1939**  Invades Albania.

**1940**  Joins war on Hitler's side; attacks France, Greece and Egypt.

**1943**  Deposed and arrested; rescued by Germans; sets up new Fascist state in northern Italy; executes opponents.

**1945**  Flees for the border; captured; executed 28 April in Milan.

# Adolf Hitler
## ◄ 1889–1945 ►
## FÜHRER OF GERMANY

Hitler is without doubt the most infamous tyrant of the 20th century, possibly of all time. Dictator of Germany for twelve years, he ordered the imprisonment and death of well over six million people. He also provoked World War II, causing between 35 and 60 million more to die and Germany to be completely destroyed and dismembered.

Born and raised in Austria, the son of a customs officer who was brutal to his wife and children, Hitler idolized his mother and aspired to become an artist. Twice failing to gain admission to the Academy of Fine Arts in Vienna, he eked out a living painting postcards and advertisements. Lonely and isolated, he began to develop megalomaniacal fantasies and a hatred of Jews.

Hitler was rejected as unfit for service by the Austrian army but, on the outbreak of World War I, he was accepted by the 16th Bavarian Reserve Infantry Regiment. A brave, even reckless soldier, he was badly wounded in 1916 and gassed at the end of the war. Decorated four times, he won the Iron Cross First Class in 1918, although he was never promoted beyond the rank of corporal.

His time in the army turned him into a militaristic nationalist and he remained with his regiment until 1920, serving as an army political agent. He left to work as head of the propaganda section of the German Workers' Party, which he had joined in 1919. He worked tirelessly for the party which, in August 1920, changed its name to the *National-sozialistische Deutsche Arbeiterpartei* – or Nazi Party.

Based in Munich, the party attracted former servicemen who felt that they had not lost the war on the battlefield but had been betrayed by communists at home, among whom there were many Jewish intellectuals. Hitler also played on the discontent caused by the punitive nature of the Treaty of Versailles that had ended the war.

With the help of Ernst Röhm, an army staff officer, Hitler was elected president of the party in July 1921. In his hypnotic oratory, Hitler attacked

Jews and communists, while Röhm organized squads of storm troopers to protect party meetings and beat up political opponents. These thugs were organized into a private army called the *Sturmabteilung*, the SA or Brownshirts.

In November 1923, Hitler staged the Munich Beer Hall Putsch, a failed attempt to take over the Bavarian government. Convicted of treason, he was sentenced to five years imprisonment. In Landsberg prison, he wrote *Mein Kampf* – 'My Struggle' – in which he outlined his political philosophy. He extolled the virtues of racial purity and the force of the will, and declared his unending opposition to Jews, communists, liberals and foreign capitalists. Germany, he said, would rise to become the world's dominant power. It would take its revenge for its defeat in World War I, unite the German speaking peoples now living in other countries and expand to the east, finding *Lebensraum*, or living space, in central Europe and Russia. It was a philosophy of tyranny.

Released after nine months, Hitler recruited air ace Herman Göring, strong-arm man Heinrich Himmler and master propagandist Josef Goebbels to the cause. The world-wide economic collapse of 1929 brought chaos to the streets that could be exploited by the Nazi storm troopers. Hitler also forged an alliance with the Nationalist Party, led by industrialist Alfred Hugenberg, increasing Nazi representation in the German parliament – the Reichstag – from 12 to 107. In the 1932 elections, this increased to 230, making the Nazis the biggest party in the Reichstag and, in January 1933, the German president, ageing war hero Paul von Hindenberg, finally agreed to appoint Hitler Reich chancellor.

When the Reichstag was burned down in February 1933 – in a fire possibly started by the Nazis themselves – Hitler found an excuse to outlaw the Communist Party and arrest its leaders. In March 1933, an Enabling Act gave Hitler dictatorial powers for four years. He used this to dismantle all other political parties, purge the government of Jews and bring all its offices under direct control of the Nazi Party. Then on 30 June 1934 – the Night of the Long Knives – he purged the party of radicals, murdering Röhm and hundreds of others who posed a threat to Hitler's domination. The SA were replaced by the *Schutzstaffel* or SS under Himmler who were loyal only to Hitler himself, and a secret police force called the Gestapo was set up.

When Hindenberg died in August 1934, Hitler took over the presidency, naming himself Führer of what he named the Third Reich. He sent Jews, political enemies and anyone else he found 'undesirable' to concentration camps set up by the SS. In 1935, the Nuremberg Racial Laws stripped Jews of citizenship and, in defiance of the Versailles Treaty, Hitler set up an air force – the Luftwaffe – started building tanks and sent troops into the demilitarized Rhineland.

In 1936, he formed the Rome-Berlin 'Axis' with Italy's Fascist dictator Benito Mussolini, and signed an anti-communist pact with Japan. In 1938, he annexed Austria and demanded that Czechoslovakia hand over the Sudetenland, a border region where the inhabitants spoke German. Unprepared for war, the Western allies sought to appease Hitler, and Britain and France agreed to the dismemberment of Czechoslovakia at the Munich Conference in September 1938. However, Hitler, not content with the Sudetenland, quickly swallowed up the rest of Czechoslovakia and began making yet more territorial demands.

*Rabble-rouser: on the eve of war 1939, Hitler addresses the masses.*

After concluding a non-aggression pact with the Soviet Union on 23 August 1939, Hitler invaded Poland on 1 September. Britain and France declared war, but there was little they could do. Poland was quickly overrun, with the eastern half being taken by the Soviet Union. Hitler then seized Denmark and Norway.

Hitler's fast-moving mechanized forces overran the Low Countries and France in a matter of weeks, but his plans to invade the United Kingdom had to be shelved when the Luftwaffe failed to gain control of the skies in the Battle of Britain.

In April 1941, he invaded Yugoslavia and Greece and, in June, he tore up the non-aggression pact and invaded the Soviet Union. Although his army won spectacular victories in the field, they failed to take Moscow before the Russian winter set in. The Russians began to exact a huge toll on the German armies, and in the winter of 1942–43 defeated the Germans at Stalingrad. Meanwhile Britain had beaten decisively Hitler's seemingly invincible mechanized forces in the deserts of North Africa.

Hitler now had another powerful enemy to face. In December 1941, the Japanese had attacked the US Pacific Fleet at its base in Pearl Harbor, Hawaii, beginning a war in the Pacific. Hitler promptly declared war on the United States.

At home, Hitler's pathological hatred of Jews resulted in the 'Final Solution'. In the Holocaust, six million Jews – along with gypsies, homo-sexuals, Slavs and other people thought to be inferior – were murdered in death camps, worked to death in labour camps or simply died from maltreatment and disease.

By 1943, the war had turned against Hitler. On the Eastern Front, the Soviet army was pushing the Germans out of Russia. Sicily had been invaded, Mussolini had fallen, Allied forces were pushing their way up the Italian peninsula, and British and American bombers were pounding German cities every night.

On 6 June 1944, Allied troops landed on the coast of Normandy. Hitler had now taken the conduct of the war into his own hands and persisted in making disastrous military blunders. A plot was hatched among a number of his senior officers and on 20 July 1944 a bomb went off under a table where he was working. It failed to kill him. Those responsible were rounded up, tortured and executed horribly.

In December 1944, Hitler staged a short-lived counter-offensive in the Ardennes. But he no longer had the manpower or the industrial might to resist the forces set against him. As the Russians and the Allies closed in on Berlin, Hitler organized a defence to the last man. Germany, he believed, deserved to be destroyed because it had failed to live up to his great vision for it. However, his courage failed him. On 29 April 1945, he married his long-term mistress Eva Braun, and the following day, the two of them committed suicide. In accordance with his instructions, their bodies were burnt.

## Life and Crimes

**1889** Born 20 April in Braunau am Inn, Austria.

**1907** Moves to Vienna to become an artist.

**1913** Moves to Munich.

**1914** Joins German army.

**1916** Seriously wounded on Western Front.

**1918** Gassed; awarded Iron Cross First Class.

**1919** Joins German Workers' Party.

**1921** Becomes president of newly renamed Nazi Party.

**1923** Attempted putsch against Bavarian government fails; jailed for treason; writes *Mein Kampf*.

**1932** Nazis become largest party in Reichstag.

**1933** Appointed Reich chancellor; jails communists; takes dictator powers.

**1934** Purges party in the Night of the Long Knives; takes over presidency, naming himself Führer of the Third Reich.

**1935** Strips Jews of citizenship; starts re-arming.

**1936** Sends troops into the Rhineland; forms Axis with Italy; signs pact with Japan.

**1938** Annexes Austria; takes over Sudetenland after being appeased by Britain and France at Munich Conference; overruns western Czechoslovakia.

**1939** Signs non-aggression pact with Stalin; invades Poland, forcing Britain and France to declare war.

**1940** Overruns Scandinavian, the Low Countries and France; defeated by the Royal Air Force in the Battle of Britain.

**1941** Overruns the Balkans and Greece; invades the Soviet Union; declares war on the US.

**1942** Defeated by the British in el Alamein. The 'Final Solution' – with Hitler's approval – is put into operation following the Wannsee Conference in Berlin.

**1943** Defeated by the Russians at Stalingrad; driven out of North Africa by the Allies, who invade Italy.

**1944** Allies land in Normandy; bomb attempt on Hitler's life fails; short-lived counter-offensive in the Ardennes.

**1945** Germany invaded; commits suicide 30 April.

# António de Oliveira Salazar
## ◄ 1889–1970 ►
## RULER OF PORTUGAL

After training for the priesthood, Salazar decided instead to become an economist and rose to become a professor at the University of Coimbra. He helped form the Catholic Centre Party in 1915, but after one term in the national assembly, stepped down, declaring the body to be useless.

In 1926, Portugal was bankrupt. The army seized power and Salazar was invited to become minister of finance. He refused, saying that the position would not give him enough power. Two years later, when he was given the power he wanted, he joined the government. He imposed massive new taxes, but each year decreased the rate of tax. It seemed to work. By 1932, he had balanced the budget and had himself appointed prime minister. In that role, the president Óscar Carmona gave him a more or less free hand.

Salazar wrote a new constitution. Under it the president would be elected for seven years, but would have dictatorial power. There would be strict censorship and opposition parties would be outlawed. In the *Estado Novo*, the single ruling party, the National Union formed in 1930, aimed to suppress public opinion rather than mobilize it, unlike the Fascist and Nazi Parties.

The new constitution was approved by a referendum in 1933. Carmona remained president, but merely as a figurehead while Salazar wielded power. The following year he exiled Francisco Rolão Preto head of the Portuguese National Syndicalists, or Blue Shirt, Portugal's fascist party.

During the Spanish Civil War and World War II, Salazar took on the portfolios of minister of war and foreign minister too, keeping Portugal out of both conflicts. In 1936, when Communist sailors took over two naval ships, confining their officers and attempted to sale out of the harbour to support the Republic cause in Spain he ordered the ships to be destroyed by gunfire.

Surviving sailors were set to the Tarrafal prison camp Salazar had established on the Cape Verde Islands for political prisoners. This was known as the 'slow death camp' because of the heat and insanitary conditions. After that, all government employees had to foreswear Communism and swear a loyalty oath.

Then in 1939, Spain and Portugal signed the Iberian Pact, which helped keep both countries out of the war. Having survived the war as a neutral, Salazar sought to liberalize the country in 1945, but when the Cold War started he cracked down again in 1948. When opposition leader, Humberto Delgado openly challenged Salazar's regime in the 1958 presidential election, he was first exiled and then killed by Salazar's secret police.

In 1968, Salazar had a stroke and was forced to leave office. He died two years later, having lived a dull, quiet and thrifty life, and never having left Portugal.

## Life and Crimes

**1889** Born 28 April, Vimieiro, Portugal.

**1914** Becomes an economist.

**1921** Founds Catholic Centre Party; elected to National Assembly.

**1928** Becomes minister of finance.

**1932** Becomes prime minister.

**1952** Takes Portugal into NATO.

**1968** Suffers debilitating stroke.

**1970** Dies 27 July in Lisbon.

# Rafael Trujillo
◀ 1891–1961 ▶

## DICTATOR OF THE DOMINICAN REPUBLIC

Rafael Trujillo ruled the Dominican Republic from 1930 until his assassination in 1961.

Born in 1891 to a lower middle-class family in San Cristóbal, Trujillo received little in the way of formal education and made his living as a part-time telegraph operator and small-time thief. In 1916, the United States occupied the Dominican Republic. Joining the Dominican army in 1918, Trujillo was trained by the US Marines. He became a lieutenant in the national police in 1919, rising to the rank of colonel by the time the US left in 1924. The following year Trujillo became head of the national police force, and in 1927 he became a general and commander of the army.

In 1930, he staged a military coup, ousting President Horacio Vásquez. Maintaining command of the army, he put members of his family in key political offices and murdered all those who opposed him. He held the title of president himself from 1930 to 1938 and 1942 to 1952, at other times allowing the office to be held by various puppets.

The Dominican Republic's one political party, the Partido Dominicano, also controlled the press. Members of congress were hand-picked by Trujillo, and competing units of secret policemen reporting directly to him effectively suppressed any political activity.

Trujillo was known as 'The Benefactor' though it was largely his family that benefited from the economic growth brought by the political stability his rule engendered. Others suffered, particularly Haitians who strayed over the border: in 1937, 20,000 migrant agricultural workers were massacred.

In spite of the harsh measures he took to protect his regime, opposition grew and he came under foreign pressure to liberalize his rule. On 31 May 1961, he was driving out to his farm in San Cristóbal, when he was cut down by machine-gun fire in a coup backed by the CIA. His eldest son took control, tracked down the supposed assassins and executed them.

However, he could not hold on to power, and was soon forced into exile with the rest of the family, taking by way of compensation an estimated $500 million with them.

# Life and Crimes

**1891** Born 24 October in San Cristóbal, Dominican Republic.

**1918** Joins Dominican army.

**1925** Heads national police.

**1927** Becomes commanding general of the army.

**1930** Ousts President Horacio Vásquez; seizes power and instigates one-party rule.

**1937** Massacres 20,000 Haitian migrant farm workers.

**1938** Leaves presidency though retains power through puppet.

**1942** Returns to office as president.

**1952** Leaves presidency but again retains power through puppet.

**1961** Assassinated 31 May.

# Francisco Franco

◄ 1892–1975 ►

## DICTATOR OF SPAIN

An ardent royalist, Francisco Paulino Hermenegildo Teódulo Franco y Bahamonde Salgado Pardo was shocked when Spain became a republic in 1931 and the king was forced to leave. Already the youngest general in the army, he rose to become chief of the general staff despite his monarchist views.

But he was still seen as a danger. When the left-wing Popular Front won the election in February 1936, he was exiled to the Canary Islands. From there he organized a Nationalist conspiracy that led to the outbreak of the Spanish Civil War. On 17 July 1936 garrisons across Spain revolted and Franco's nationalists took control of Morocco, then a Spanish colony, the Balearic Islands with the exception of Minorca and much of northern Spain.

Franco flew to Morocco and airlifted the large garrison of Spanish Foreign Legion troops there to mainland Spain and marched on Madrid, which they besieged. On 29 September 1936, the Nationalists established their own government at Burgos, with Franco at its head. The following year, he became head of the Nationalist Falange Party.

With the aid of the Nazi German Legion Kondor and Fascist Italy's Corpo Truppe Volontgari, he ground down the Loyalists, who were backed by the Soviet Union, France, Mexico and a volunteer International Brigade. There were atrocities on both sides. It is estimated that more than fifty thousand were executed, murdered or assassinated. The Germans used the war to try out new tactics that they would employ during World War II, most notably carpet bombing the undefended Basque market town of Guernica.

By February 1939, nearly half-a-million Spaniards had fled across the border into France. The Republican government fled into exile on 5 March. Two days later fighting broke out between communist and non-communist forces in Madrid. Franco moved in for the kill. Madrid fell to the Nationalists on 28 March 1939 and the Republican forces disbanded.

It is estimated that half-a-million were killed in the Spanish Civil War, with another half-a-million dead from starvation and disease.

With the end of the Civil War, Franco became dictator of Spain. He outlawed all opposition parties and imprisoned and executed thousands of Loyalists. However, he managed to keep Spain out of World War II, though he did send workers to aid industrial production in Germany and the Spanish volunteer División Azul, or Blue Brigade, fought on the Russian Front. He also provided facilities for German ships.

Lacking any strong ideology, Franco sought support from the royalist Carlists, the National Syndicalists and the National Catholic Party. These were combined in a single ruling coalition called the Movimiento Nacional, which was so heterogeneous that it lacked the strict ideology of the German Nazi Party or the Italian Fascists. It was a conservative, traditionalist, rightist regime that emphasized order and stability, rather than a social or political vision.

Although he was a monarchist, Franco left the throne vacant and usurped royal powers. He wore the uniform of a captain general, a rank traditionally reserved for the king in Spain. He lived in the Prado Palace and adopted the kingly privilege of walking beneath a canopy.

His official titles were Jefe del Estado – Chief of State – and Generalísimo de los Ejércitos Españoles – Highest General of the Spanish Armed Forces. But he also took as his personal title por la gracia de Dios, Caudillo de España y de la Cruzada, or 'by the grace of God, Caudillo of Spain and of the Crusade' – 'by the grace of God' is legal phraseology only used by monarchs.

During his rule, non-government trade unions and all opposition political parties – including communists, anarchists, liberal democrats and Basque and Catalan nationalists – were suppressed. Freemasons were also outlawed as Franco believed they were conspiring against him.

After World War II, Franco made a show of liberal reforms, introducing a bill of rights and promising to restore the monarchy. During the Cold War his anti-communist stance made him an ally of the United States. In 1953, an alliance was concluded which allowed the US to establish air bases on Spanish territory, and in 1955, with the backing of the US, Falangist Spain was admitted to the United Nations.

During the 1960s, he reversed many of his liberal stances, repressing unrest among the Basques, workers, students and the clergy. In July 1969, he chose Juan Carlos de Bourbon, grandson of the previous king, as heir to the throne, who succeeded when Franco died in 1975.

# Life and Crimes

**1892**  Born 4 December in El Ferrol, Spain.

**1907**  Enrols in military academy.

**1912**  Fights in war in Morocco.

**1920**  Appointed deputy command of the Spanish Foreign Legion in Morocco.

**1921–1926**  Fights in Riff Rebellion.

**1923**  Promoted commander of the Foreign Legion.

**1926**  Becomes Spain's youngest brigadier general.

**1928**  Appointed director of the military academy.

**1934**  Suppresses miners' revolt, earning respect of right, hatred of left.

**1935**  Named chief of the general staff.

**1936**  Exiled to Canaries; returns with Foreign Legion; establishes Nationalist government with himself at its head.

**1937**  Becomes leader of ruling Falange Party.

**1939**  Defeats Loyalists, imprisoning and executing thousands.

**1947**  Promises return of monarchy.

**1953**  Allows US to establish military bases in Spain.

**1969**  Names Juan Carlos as heir to the throne.

**1975**  Dies 20 November in Madrid.

# Ayatollah Khomeini
## ◀ 1900–1989 ▶
### RULER OF IRAN

Exiled from Iran in 1964 for leading a religious movement against the rule of the Shah of Iran, the Shi'ite cleric Ayatollah Ruhollah Khomeini returned from France in triumph in January 1979, after the Shah had been ousted. In December, he was named political and religious leader of the Islamic Republic of Iran for life.

With his grey beard and black turban and robes, the dour cleric portrayed himself as the avenger of all the humiliations that the West had heaped on the Muslim world over the centuries. He rejected not just the rule of the Shah, but also the secularism it embodied.

Born Ruhollah Musami to a family of Shi'ite scholars in the village of Khomeyn near Tehran in 1900, his given name means 'inspired of God' and throughout his life he was acclaimed for his depth of religious learning. When he was five months old, his father was killed on the orders of a local landlord. He was raised by his mother and aunt, then by his older brothers. After studying in various Islamic schools, he settled in the city of Qom in 1922 and took the name of his home town as his surname.

Like his father before him, Khomeini started his career as a theologian, then became an Islamic jurist. He wrote extensively on Islamic philosophy, ethics and law, but he took little part in politics when the first Shah of modern times, Reza Shah Pahlavi, secularized the Iranian state, or when his son Mohammad Reza Pahlavi turned to the Americans to save his regime when protestors clamoured for democratic reform on the streets of Tehran. In the mid-1950s, he was acclaimed as an ayatollah or religious leader.

Khomeini was a follower of Iran's pre-eminent cleric, Ayatollah Mohammed Boroujerdi, who preached traditional Islamic deference to state power. But after Boroujerdi's death in 1962, Khomeini spoke out, attacking the Shah for his ties with Israel and warned that the Jews were aiming to take over the country. He denounced a bill giving the vote to women as anti-Islamic, opposed land reform that would break up religious estates and condemned the proposal that allowed American servicemen stationed in Iran to be tried in US military courts as 'a document for Iran's enslavement'. For him America was the 'Great Satan'. His religious zeal and his anti-Western stance won him a large following in Iran and his arrest in 1963 sparked anti-government riots.

After a year's imprisonment the Shah exiled him to Turkey, hoping that he would be forgotten. But Khomeini moved to the Shi'ite holy city of An-Najaf in central Iraq where he was revered. Cassette tapes of his sermons smuggled back to Iran were peddled in the bazaars and he became the most prominent leader of the exiled opposition.

In An-Najaf, Khomeini fundamentally changed the face of Shi'ism, which had previous sought only to guide the state. Condemning the Shah's servility to the Americans, and his secularism, Khomeini called for the establishment of a theocratic state, something which had no precedent in Islam.

*The Iranian army demonstrates its support for the Ayatollah, 1979.*

In 1978 huge street demonstrations shook the Iranian regime and in January 1979 the Shah fled to Egypt. Khomeini was then settled near Neuf-le-Château, a suburb of Paris. Two weeks after the Shah's fall, he returned to Iran in triumph. Popularly acclaimed as leader, Khomeini set out to confirm his authority and to lay the groundwork for a clerical state. With revolutionary fervour riding high, armed vigilante bands and kangaroo courts made bloody work of the Shah's last partisans, executing hundreds.

Khomeini closed the new parliament, suppressed all opposition and ordered an Assembly of Experts to draft an Islamic constitution. Overruling reservations from the Shi'ite hierarchy, the delegates designed a state that would be run by Khomeini with the clergy enforcing religious law. Those who opposed him were systematically imprisoned and killed. Women were forced to wear the veil. Alcohol and Western music were banned and the brutal punishments required by Islamic law were enforced.

On 4 November 1979, 500 of his student supporters took over the United States embassy and held 52 Americans hostage there for more than a year. Over the following decade, Khomeini consolidated his rule. He was every bit as ruthless as the Shah and killed thousands stamping out a rebellion of the secular left. The ministries of the state were packed with clerics and the media and schools recited his personal doctrines. He also purged the security services and the military, rebuilding them with men loyal to the clerical state.

Khomeini also launched a campaign to export his Islamic revolution to other Muslim countries. His provocations of Iraq in 1980 helped start the Iran–Iraq war which cost a million lives. He refused to countenance any peaceful solution. The war only ended after America intervened and sank several Iranian warships in the Persian Gulf. Khomeini described the ceasefire as 'more deadly than taking poison' to him.

With the Iranian economy on its knees and a entire generation of young men wiped out, Iranians asked whether God had revoked his blessing of the revolution. To rally his demoralized supporters, Khomeini issued a *fatwa* condemning the writer Salman Rushdie to death for heresy over his novel *The Satanic Verses*. Though born a Muslim, Rushdie was not a Shi'ite and he was a British subject born in India with no ties to Iran. With the *fatwa* [an Islamic religious edict, not, as was widely believed in the West at the time, a death sentence], Khomeini claimed authority over Muslims worldwide, insisting that Islam was not an outdated force confined to Arabia but was everywhere and for all time

Khomeini died a few months later in June 1989, leaving his country in the hands of other stern theocrats. But the *fatwa* lived on, a source of bitterness between Iran and the West as Khomeini surely intended it to be. His other legacy was the growing appeal of an Islamic state and of fundamentalism, which inspired the Taleban and Osama bin Laden.

## Life and Crimes

| | |
|---|---|
| **1900** | Born 17 May in Khomeyn, Iran. |
| **1911** | Takes the name of his home town as his surname. |
| **1950s** | Becomes an ayatollah, or religious leader. |
| **1960s** | Takes title grand ayatollah. |
| **1962–1963** | Speaks out against the shah. |
| **1964** | Forced into exile in Paris. |
| **1979** | Returns in triumph to form government; kills those who stand against him; masterminds seizing of US embassy hostages. |
| **1980** | Iran–Iraq war begins. |
| **1988** | Ceasefire ends war after it has been fought to a stalemate. |
| **1989** | Dies 3 June in Tehran. |

# Fulgencio Batista y Zaldívar
## ◄ 1901–1973 ►
### DICTATOR OF CUBA

Fulgencio Batista y Zaldívar is now best known for the fact that he was deposed by the young revolutionary Fidel Castro, who went on to become a tyrant himself.

Born 16 January 1901 the son of an impoverished farmer, Batista joined the army in 1921. In September 1933, he organized the 'sergeant's revolt' which toppled the provisional government of Carlos Manuel de Cespedes who had replaced the previous dictator Gerardo Machado y Morales. Rather than taking power himself, Batista controlled a series of civilian puppet presidents while pulling the strings in the background as army chief of staff until 1940, when he was elected president himself.

He began a huge programme of public works and greatly expanded the economy – allowing the Mafia, under New York gangster Meyer Lansky, to run the casinos there. Under Lansky's criminal guidance, Cuba became a resort island for the United States, famed for its music, cigars, rum and relaxed attitude to prostitution. Batista enriched himself with kickbacks and, at the end of his first presidential term in 1944, retired to Florida a wealthy man.

In 1952, he returned to Cuba, seizing power in a bloodless coup again. Two years later he was confirmed in office by popular elections and was re-elected again in 1958. However, his second period in office was marked by brutal repression, with Batista controlling the press, the universities and the Congress with an iron fist, all the while embezzling huge sums from the soaring economy.

The widespread corruption led to the growth of a guerrilla movement under Castro. Batista's flagrant abuse of power led US President Dwight D. Eisenhower to ban the sale of arms to Cuba. Without American backing, Batista could not resist Castro's forces and on 1 January 1959, he fled to the Dominican Republic. He lived comfortably in exile on the island of Madeira and in Estoril, near Lisbon, dying in Marbella, Spain on 6 August 1973.

# Life and Crimes

**1901**  Born 16 January in Banes, Cuba.

**1921**  Joins the Cuban army.

**1933**  Stages 'sergeant's revolt' and rules Cuba from behind the scenes as army chief of staff.

**1940**  Elected president.

**1944**  Retires to Florida a wealthy man.

**1952**  Returns to power in Cuba after bloodless coup.

**1958**  Castro's guerrillas make first significant gains.

**1959**  Batista flees into exile.

**1973**  Dies 6 August in Spain.

# Ngo Dinh Diem
◄ 1901–1963 ►
## PRESIDENT OF SOUTH VIETNAM

Ngo Dinh Diem was the US-backed president of South Vietnam from 1954 to 1963, who sought to prove his anti-communist credentials by brutal repression.

Born to one of Vietnam's noble families, he went to Catholic school in the ancient imperial capital Hue and studied for the civil service at college in Hanoi, where he met Vo Nguyen Giap who went on to lead the victorious communist forces. In 1933, Diem served as minister of the interior in the government of the Emperor Bao Dai, but resigned when the colonial power, France, refused to give Vietnam more autonomy.

For the next 12 years, he shunned public life. But in 1945, he was captured by the communist forces who had been fighting the Japanese. The Communist leader Ho Chi Minh invited him to join the government he had established in Hanoi in the hope that Diem's presence would attract the support of other Catholics. Diem refused and went into self-imposed exile in the United States, where he met John F. Kennedy, then a senator from Massachusetts.

In 1954, Vietnam had been temporarily divided by the Geneva Peace Accords which had ended the French Indochina War. With Ho Chi Minh's Communist government in control in the north, Bao Dai invited Diem to return as prime minister in his US-backed regime in the south. Diem accepted, then pushed the emperor aside in a fraudulent referendum in 1955, declaring himself president of the Republic of Vietnam, known as South Vietnam.

The Geneva Accords stipulated that there should be an election to unite the two halves of the country. Fearing that the Communists would win, Diem refused to hold one and called on the US to back him with economic and military aid. Meanwhile he ruthlessly repressed political dissenters and religious factions, and installed members of his family in important jobs.

Favouring Catholics he alienated the Buddhists that made up the majority of the population. His inept war against communist insurgency further alienated the peasantry, and a failed coup attempt in 1960 sparked more brutal repression. Hundreds of Buddhists were killed in a violent confrontation. This prompted the US to withdraw its support from his regime – inviting another coup. Diem was overthrown by the army on 1 November 1963. The following day he and his brother were shot in Cho Lon, South Vietnam.

# Life and Crimes

**1901** Born 3 January Quang Binh province, northern Vietnam.

**1933** Serves as minister of the interior in Emperor Bao Dai's government.

**1945** Captured by Communists and invited to join Ho Chi Minh's government; refuses and goes into exile.

**1954** Returns as prime minister in Bao Dai's government in South Vietnam.

**1955** Ousts Bao Dai in fixed election; declares a republic and names himself president.

**1960** Responds to failed coup with brutal repression, killing hundreds of Buddhists on the grounds they are aiding the Communist North.

**1963** Ousted in coup; assassinated 2 November in Cho Lon, South Vietnam.

# Sukarno
## ◀ 1901–1970 ▶
## PRESIDENT OF INDONESIA

Indonesia was an old Dutch colony and during the 1920s and 1930s, Sukarno came to prominence as a nationalist politician seeking independence. As a result, he spent two years in a Dutch prison and eight in exile.

When the Japanese invaded during World War II, Sukarno welcomed them as liberators, acting as their chief adviser and recruiting labour, soldiers and 'comfort women' – otherwise known as sex slaves – for them.

At the end of the war, Sukarno was persuaded to declare Indonesia's independence. The Dutch were finally forced to concede sovereignty in 1949 and Sukarno quickly established himself in the governor-general's lavish palace.

He easily won the first presidential election, but his government was notoriously corrupt. After extracting a billion dollars' worth of aid from the US, he switched sides in the Cold War and took a billion dollars from the Soviet Union. Meanwhile inflation soared. In 1959 he dissolved parliament and in 1963 made himself president for life.

*Sukarno on an official state visit to Kuwait, 1962.*

He became increasingly fearful of a military coup and in 1965 he approved a communist-backed plot to kidnap six top army generals who were then tortured, mutilated and murdered. General Suharto, commander of the Jakarta garrison, reacted by slaughtering more than 300,000 communist suspects. Suharto gradually took over power, forcing Sukarno to retire in 1968, and installed himself as president. Whether life in Indonesia became any better under Suharto is a moot point.

## Life and Crimes

**1901**  Born 6 June in Surabaja, Java.
**1928**  Founds Indonesian Nationalist Party.
**1942**  Welcomes Japanese invaders, becoming chief collaborator.
**1945**  Declares independence.
**1949**  Dutch cede sovereignty; Sukarno takes power.
**1959**  Dissolves parliament.
**1963**  Declares himself president for life.
**1965**  Implicated in coup against the army.
**1966**  Cedes wide powers to Suharto.
**1968**  Stands down as president.
**1970**  Dies of kidney failure on 21 June in Jakarta, Indonesia.

# François Duvalier ('Papa Doc')
## ◀ 1907–1971 ▶
## PRESIDENT OF HAITI

François Duvalier earned his nickname 'Papa Doc' as a rural physician who worked tirelessly to eradicate malaria and yaws during an epidemic in Haiti in the 1940s. At the same time he became involved in a writers' group which explored black nationalism and voodoo.

After serving as minister of health, he became president in a rigged election in 1957, ostensibly winning the biggest majority in Haitian history. He then set about consolidating his power, employing a ruthless group of thugs called the 'Tonton Macoutes' – or 'Bogeymen' – to terrorize the populace and assassinate suspected opponents of the regime.

After his chief aide, Clément Barbot, deputized for him when he had a heart attack, Duvalier had him imprisoned then murdered. The US withdrew its aid after Duvalier had his term of office illegally extended. He simply amended the 1957 constitution that had prevented a president standing for a second term. In 1963, he was re-elected, seemingly without a single vote against him.

In 1964, he was declared president for life. This was passed in a referendum by a similarly implausible majority. The amended constitution also gave him absolute power and the right to name his successor.

Haiti was shunned by other nations and Duvalier was excommunicated by the Pope in 1966 for harassing the clergy. But he held on to power using a mixture of voodoo and strong-arm gangster tactics, always keeping a pearl-handed pistol, loaded, on his desk in the presidential palace.

Duvalier ordered the head of an executed rebel packed in ice and brought to him so he could commune with the dead man's spirit. Peepholes were drilled in the walls of the interrogation chambers, so Duvalier could watch detainees being tortured and submerged in baths of sulphuric acid. That was when he wasn't in the torture room himself.

Duvalier misappropriated millions of dollars of international aid, including the $15 million that the United States had supplied annually. It simply disappeared into his personal account, along with the property of anyone suspected of having Communist sympathies.

The mulatto elite fled abroad leaving a shortage of doctors and teachers. Land held by the peasants was given to the militia who, with no official salary, sustained themselves through crime and extortion. Meanwhile the dispossessed fled to the slums where malnutrition and famine were endemic.

When Duvalier died in 1971, he was succeeded by his 19-year-old son Jean-Claude 'Baby Doc' Duvalier. The US put pressure on Baby Doc to soften the tyrannical regime of his father, but the corruption was endemic and the Tontons Macoutes would not mend their ways. Popular protest turned into open rebellion in November 1985. On 7 February 1986, a US Air Force jet carried Baby Doc and his wife into exile in France.

## Life and Crimes

**1907**　Born 14 April in Port-au-Prince, Haiti.
**1934**　Graduates from University of Haiti School of Medicine.
**1943**　Joins US-backed anti-yaws campaign.
**1946**　Heads National Public Heath Service.
**1949**　Becomes minister of health.
**1957**　Elected president in fraudulent election.
**1959**　Imprisons deputy, later murdering him.
**1961**　Fixes legislative elections; extends term of office; loses US aid.
**1963**　Begins cult of personality.
**1964**　Becomes president for life.
**1966**　Excommunicated for harassing clergy.
**1971**　Dies 21 April, Port-au-Prince.
**1986**　Son Baby Doc flees into exile.

# Enver Hoxha
## ◄ 1908–1985 ►
## LEADER OF ALBANIA

Born to a Muslim family in southern Albania, Enver Hoxha won a scholarship to study in France where he became a communist. He had returned to Albania when his country was invaded by the Italians in 1939 and set up a tobacco shop in the capital Tirana, which became a front for the resistance.

When the Communist Party of Albania was formed in 1941, he became general secretary and political commissar of the Communist-dominated Army of National Liberation. When the Germans left in 1944, he set up a provisional government and began trials of those accused of collaborating. Those found guilty were executed, ridding him of a number of political enemies. And when Yugoslavia broke with the Soviet Union in 1948, Hoxha purged the party of pro-Tito Communists.

A Stalinist, Hoxha fell out with Stalin's successor Khrushchev and aligned Albania with Mao Tse-tung's China. At home, he confiscated private property and closed churches and mosques. He herded the people into collective farms and newly-built factories. Anyone who resisted was exiled, imprisoned or shot. Even so, his efforts to develop the country failed.

Following the death of Mao Tse-tung, relations with China soured. Now an international pariah, Hoxha declared that Albania would become a socialist paradise on its own. In 1981, to ensure the succession of a younger generation of communists, he ordered the execution of a number of government and party leaders. He died in 1985 after 40 years in power. Soon after, the Communist Party itself was ousted.

## Life and Crimes

**1908**  Born 16 October in Gjirokastër, Albania.
**1930**  Goes to France to study engineering.

**1934** Serves as secretary in Albanian consulate in Brussels.

**1936** Returns to Albania to become a teacher.

**1939** Dismissed for refusing to join Albanian Fascist Party; opens tobacconist's.

**1941** Founds Albanian Communist Party; becomes general secretary.

**1944** Heads up provisional government; starts show trials.

**1948** Purges party of Titoists; closes churches and confiscates private property.

**1961** Breaks with Soviet Union.

**1978** Breaks with China.

**1981** Culls party and government leaders.

**1985** Dies 11 April in Tirana.

# Alfredo Stroessner
## ◀ 1912–2006 ▶
## DICTATOR OF PARAGUAY

General Alfredo Stroessner kept an iron grip on Paraguay for 35 years in the longest unbroken rule by one individual in South America in the 20th century.

Born in Encarnación, Paraguay, the son of a German beer-maker, Stroessner entered the national military school at the age of 16 and received his commission in 1932. By 1940, he had risen to the rank of major and joined the general staff in 1946.

When civil war broke out in 1947, he initially remained loyal to President Higinio Morínago, then backed Felipe Molas Lopez in a successful coup against Morínago. He then backed Federico Chávez against Lopez and by 1951 he was army chief of staff. In 1954, he ousted Chávez, becoming president after winning an election in which he was the sole candidate.

An arch anti-communist, Stroessner had the backing of the United States. His supporters packed the legislature and ran the courts, and he ruthlessly suppressed all political opposition. The constitution had to be modified in 1967 and 1977 to legitimize his six consecutive elections to the presidency. In 1988, he won an unprecedented eighth term on a

*Stroessner was one in a line of dictators who inflicted themselves on the unfortunate Paraguayans.*

majority, according to official figures, of between 90 and 98 per cent of the registered vote.

However, when the Pope visited Paraguay later that year, Stroessner provoked controversy by preventing the pontiff from meeting opposition leaders. Meanwhile, he assured John Paul II that Paraguay was a peaceful, law-abiding democracy – a claim he repeated before the United Nations in New York. He returned home to find the country in uproar. But instead of a popular revolution, Paraguay suffered another military coup led by strongman General Andres Rodriguez. Stroessner was forced into exile in Brazil, where he spent the last 17 years of his life. Following a bout of pneumonia, he tried to return to his homeland to die, but was staunchly rejected by the government, and died in Brasilia of a stroke on 16 August 2006.

## Life and Crimes

**1912**  Born 3 November in Encarnación, Paraguay.

**1928**  Enters military school.

**1940**  Rises to rank of major.

**1946**  Joins army's general staff.

**1947**  Backs President Higinio Morínago in civil war, later betraying him.

**1954**  Ousts President Federico Chávez on 5 May and takes over as president.

**1967 and 1977**  Alters constitution to permit the continuation of his presidency.

**1988**  Wins election with vote of over 90 per cent.

**1989**  Ousted in military coup.

**2006**  Dies in exile in Brazil.

# Augusto Pinochet

## ◀ 1915–2006 ▶

## PRESIDENT OF CHILE

After seizing power in a bloody CIA-backed coup, General Augusto Pinochet ruled Chile with a rod of iron for two decades, during which human rights violations became the norm of Chilean life.

Hailing from an upper middle-class background, Pinochet entered the military academy in Santiago at the age of 18, graduating three years later as a second lieutenant. By 1968 he had risen to the rank of brigadier general.

In 1970, Salvador Allende, a Marxist, became president of Chile with the backing of the Christian Democrats, and began restructuring Chilean society along socialist lines. In the process he expropriated the US-owned copper-mining companies, alienating the US government and foreign investors. He further annoyed Washington by establishing relations with Cuba and Communist China, which the United States did not recognize at that time. As a result, America imposed tough economic sanctions and the CIA spent millions of dollars destabilizing the Allende regime, much of it going into Pinochet's pockets.

By 1972, the Chilean economy had collapsed. With no foreign investment, production had come to a standstill. There were widespread strikes, runaway inflation, food shortages and civil unrest. With the backing of the armed forces, Pinochet staged a military coup on 11 September 1973. It was bloody even by Latin American standards. The navy seized the key port of Valparaíso, while the army surrounded the presidential palace in Santiago. Allende refused to step down. When the palace was overrun a few hours later, he was found dead. It appears that he shot himself rather than face inevitable torture and execution.

A junta took over and declared martial law. Those who violated the curfew were shot on sight. Pinochet was named president two days later. He broke off relations with Cuba – Nixon had staged his famous rapprochement with China by then – and moved against Allende's supporters.

Some 14,000 would be tried and executed or expelled from the country, while Pinochet claimed he was only trying to 'restore institutional normality' to Chile.

In June 1974 Pinochet assumed sole power, with the rest of the junta relegated to an advisory role. Under Pinochet's tyrannical rule, it is estimated that 20,000 people were killed and torture was widespread.

While Pinochet continued to maintain tight control over the political opposition, he was rejected by a plebiscite in 1988. He eventually stepped down in 1990 after securing immunity from prosecution in Chile. He stayed on as army chief of staff. However, during a shopping trip to London in October 1998, he was arrested on a Spanish warrant charging him with murder. He was later accused of torture and human rights violations. For 16 months, he fought his extradition through the British courts. In January 2000, Home Secretary Jack Straw decided that he was too ill to stand trial and sent him back to Chile. He died in 2006.

## Life and Crimes

**1915** Born 25 November in Valparaíso, Chile.

**1936** Graduates from military academy.

**1973** Stages coup against the elected government of Salvador Allende.

**1974** Assumes sole power.

**1978** His murderous rule endorsed by 75 per cent vote in plebiscite.

**1981** Introduces new constitution which guarantees his presidency for a further eight years.

**1988** Rejected by a vote of 55 per cent to 43 per cent.

**1990** Steps down.

**1998** Arrested in London for murder.

**2000** Returned to Chile a free man.

**2006** Dies 10 January in Santiago.

# Ferdinand Marcos
## ◄ 1917–1989 ►
## PRESIDENT OF THE PHILIPPINES

A trained lawyer, Marcos was convicted of assassinating a political opponent of his father in 1939 and, from his condemned cell, argued his case up to the Philippine Surpreme Court, where he won an acquittal.

During World War II, Marcos collaborated with the Japanese who occupied the Philippines – though he later claimed to have led the Filipino resistance, a fiction in which the United States colluded, awarding him medals. He emerged from the war a wealthy man and served in the Philippine house of representatives and the senate, switching parties when it suited him.

Elected president in 1965, he won a second term in 1969. But in 1972, he declared martial law, imprisoned his political opponents, dissolved congress, suspended habeas corpus and used the army as his private police force. He then wrote a new constitution giving himself considerably more power. His wife, Imelda, and other family members were given lucrative government posts. While the Filipino people lived in abject poverty, the Marcoses flaunted their extravagant lifestyle, Imelda becoming world-renowned for her huge collection of shoes. (While the acquisition of shoes may no doubt be a laudable enterprise, especially from a shoe manufacturer's point of view, it is perhaps questionable whether it merits keeping an entire population in misery.)

In 1981, Marcos ended martial law, but continued to rule by decree. Opposition leader Benigno Aquino, who had gone into exile after being imprisoned for eight years by Marcos, returned in 1983, but was shot dead on the orders of Imelda in front of a plane full of journalists after he had landed at Manila. This sparked riots. An official enquiry blamed a high ranking general Fabian Ver. A family friend of the Marcoses, Ver was acquitted when the case went to court.

To reassert his authority, Marcos held an election. Benigno Aquino's widow Corazon ran against him. Marcos was declared the winner, but

*Ferdinand and Imelda Marcos. The Marcoses led an extravagant lifestyle while the people of the Philippines struggled to make ends meet.*

only after 30 election officials walked out in protest at voting fraud. Marcos quickly arrested his opponents, provoking more rioting as Aquino was widely thought to have won the election. On 25 February 1986 both Marcos and Aquino were inaugurated in competing ceremonies. The following evening Marcos accepted the United States' offer to fly him and his wife to exile in Hawaii.

After they were gone, it was discovered that they had embezzled millions of dollars. But Marcos was deemed too ill to stand trial and died on 28 September 1989. Imelda was acquitted of racketeering by a US federal court in 1990, but in 1993 was convicted of corruption by a Philippine court.

# Life and Crimes

**1917** Born 11 September in Sarrat, Philippines.

**1939** Found guilty of murder.

**1940** Acquitted by Supreme Court.

**1942–1945** Collaborates with Japanese during World War II.

**1946–1947** Assistant to president of the Philippines.

**1949–1959** Serves in house of representatives.

**1959–1965** Serves in senate; senate president 1963.

**1965** Changes party to win nomination; elected president; supports US in Vietnam war.

**1972** Declares martial law; imprisons political opponents.

**1981** Suspends martial law, but rules by decree.

**1983** Opposition leader Benigno Aquino gunned down on Imelda's orders.

**1986** 'Wins' election by massive voting fraud; goes into exile in Hawaii.

**1989** Dies 28 September in Honolulu.

**1993** Imelda convicted of corruption by Philippine court.

# Nicolae Ceausescu

## ◄ 1918–1989 ►

## DICTATOR OF ROMANIA

Nicolae Ceausescu was the hardline Communist leader of Romania whose tyrannical rule kept the country in poverty for 25 years.

Ceausescu became a Communist at the age of 18. During World War II, he was imprisoned with the influential Communist leader Gheorghe Gheorghiu-Dej, while his wife Elena, also a professed Communist, openly fraternized with Nazi officers.

When the Red Army entered Romania in 1944, Ceausescu became secretary of the Union of Communist Youth. Shortly after a Communist government was installed in 1947, he became minister of agriculture.

In 1950, he became deputy minister of defence and took the rank of major general. Then when Gheorghiu-Dej came to power in 1952, Ceausescu became his deputy. Succeeding Gheorghiu-Dej in 1965, he became first secretary of the Communist Party, then general secretary of the Communist Party. In 1967 he became president of the state council and head of state as well.

In foreign policy Ceausescu kept his distance from Moscow. Domestically his regime was as oppressive as any in the Soviet bloc. His feared secret police, the Securitate, stamped out any opposition and maintained ruthless control of the press and the media. Like the Soviet Union in the 1930s, Ceausescu embarked on a crash programme of industrialization, which built up massive foreign debts. To pay these off, he exported most of Romania's food supply: the result – famine.

He also oversaw a massive building programme, which demolished ancient Romanian villages and replaced them with soulless Soviet-style apartment blocks. Large areas of the Romanian capital Bucharest were demolished to build palaces for the Ceausescus.

Meanwhile the impoverished Romanians had to suffer a megalo-maniacal cult of personality surrounding Ceausescu and his wife. Family members were give lucrative government posts and their loathsome son Nicu raped his way around Bucharest with impunity.

*Ceausescu addresses his puppet parliament, circa 1985. Come the revolution, he and his wife were the first against the wall.*

Despite ruthless oppression, opposition grew. On 17 December 1989, Ceausescu ordered his secret police to fire on anti-government demonstrators in the city of Timisoara. Far from quelling opposition, demonstrations spread to Bucharest and Ceausescu found himself shouted down while making a speech – something that had never happened before.

On 22 December the Romanian army deserted him and sided with the demonstrators. Ceausescu and his wife tried to flee the capital in a helicopter but were captured. On 25 December they were tried by a military tribunal, convicted of mass murder and other crimes, and shot by a firing squad. Four days later Romania ceased to be a communist state and five months after that the first free elections for over 50 years were held.

# Life and Crimes

**1918** Born 26 January at Scornicesti, Romania.

**1936** Joins Communist Party.

**1939** Marries Elena Petrescu.

**1940** Imprisoned for Communist activities.

**1944** Becomes secretary of the Union of Communist Youth.

**1948** Becomes minister of agriculture.

**1950** Becomes deputy minister of defence.

**1952** Becomes deputy leader of Communist Party.

**1965** Becomes first secretary, then general secretary of Communist Party.

**1967** Becomes president of the state council and head of state.

**1974** Takes newly created post of president of Romania.

**1982** Export drive to pay off foreign debt causes famine.

**1989** Falls from power; convicted of mass murder and shot.

# Jean Bedel Bokassa

### ◀ 1921–1996 ▶

## PRESIDENT, CENTRAL AFRICAN REPUBLIC

Born in French Equatorial Africa, the son of a village chief, Jean Bedel Bokassa was orphaned at the age of 12. Educated in mission schools, he joined the French colonial army in 1939 as a private. He distinguished himself in the war in Indochina, winning medals and rising to the rank of captain.

When French Equatorial Africa gained its independence as the Central African Republic in 1960, the new president David Dacko invited Bokassa to head the armed forces. In 1966, Bokassa used his position to oust Dacko and declared himself president.

He began a reign of terror, taking all important government posts for himself. He personally supervised judicial beatings and introduced his own version of the 'three-strikes-and-you're-out rule' – thieves would have an ear cut off for the first two offences and a hand for the third.

In 1977, in emulation of his hero Napoleon, he crowned himself emperor of the Central African Empire in a ceremony costing $200 million, practically bankrupting the country. His diamond-encrusted crown alone cost $5 million.

His rule then became even more tyrannical. In 1979, he had hundreds of schoolchildren arrested for refusing to wear uniforms made in a factory he owned. He personally supervised the massacre of 100 of the children by his Imperial Guard.

*Emperor without an empire: Bokassa during his coronation, 1977, seated on a somewhat gaudy throne.*

On 20 September 1979, French paratroopers deposed him and re-installed Dacko as president. Bokassa went into exile in France where he had chateaux and other property bought with loot he had embezzled. In his absence, he was tried and sentenced to death. Inexplicably, he returned to the Central African Republic in 1986 and was put on trial. In 1987, he was cleared of charges of cannibalism, but found guilty of the murder of schoolchildren and other crimes. The death sentence was later commuted to life in solitary confinement, but just six years later, in 1993, he was freed. He died in 1996.

# Life and Crimes

**1921**  Born 22 February at Bobangui, Oubangui-Chari, French Equatorial Africa.

**1939**  Joins French army.

**1960**  Becomes army commander in the newly independent Central African Republic.

**1966**  Stages military coup and makes himself president.

**1977**  Crowns himself emperor in a ceremony that practically bankrupts the country.

**1979**  Murders 100 schoolchildren; ousted by French troops.

**1986**  Returns to Central African Republic.

**1987**  Found guilty of murder.

**1993**  Freed.

**1996**  Dies 3 November in Bangui, capital of the Central African Republic.

# Idi Amin
### ◄ 1924–2003 ►
## PRESIDENT OF UGANDA

A member of the small Kakwa tribe, Idi Amin Dada Oumee joined the British Army in 1943. He fought in Burma during World War II and in Kenya during the Mau-Mau revolt. He was also heavyweight boxing champion of Uganda and a world-class rugby player.

When Uganda gained its independence in 1962, he became chief of the army and air force. In 1971 he staged a military coup, ousting President Milton Obote and making himself president. He promoted himself to field marshal in 1975 and became life president in 1976, saying in a radio interview: 'I myself consider myself... to be the most important figure in the world.'

Mocked around the world for his pretension – he claimed to be victor over the British Empire, and a Scottish laird – behind the fancy uniforms he was a murderous thug. He murdered the husbands and boyfriends of

*Ex-British Army sergeant Idi Amin went on to promote himself a few more times.*

any woman he fancied, keeping body parts in a fridge. And he killed his own wives and lovers if he suspected adultery. His troops were allowed a similar latitude, and rape was commonplace. Larger tribes were persecuted and it is estimated that between 100,000 and 300,000 Ugandans were tortured and murdered during his reign.

In 1972 he expelled all Ugandans of Asian descent, leading to the collapse of the country's economy. He allied himself with Muammar al-Gadaffi in Libya and supported the Palestine Liberation Organization when it hijacked a French airliner carrying Jewish and Israeli passengers to Entebbe in July 1976.

In October 1978, Tanzanian troops, backed by Ugandan units who had fled over the border, invaded, reaching the capital Kampala on 13 April 1979. Amin fled to Libya, then settled in Saudia Arabia, where he lived in exile until his death in 2003.

## Life and Crimes

| | |
|---|---|
| **1924 or 1925** | Born in Koboko, Uganda. |
| **1943** | Joins King's African Rifles. |
| **1962** | Becomes chief of army and air force after Ugandan independence. |
| **1971** | Ousts Milton Obote in coup; becomes president. |
| **1972** | Expels Ugandan Asians, crippling the economy. |
| **1975** | Promotes himself to field marshal. |
| **1976** | Becomes life president; allows airliner hijacked by PLO to land at Entebbe. |
| **1978** | Ugandan nationalist troops backed by Tanzania invade. |
| **1979** | Amin flees Kampala on 13 April. |
| **2003** | Dies in exile in Saudi Arabia. |

# Francisco Macías Nguema
◀ 1924–1979 ▶

## PRESIDENT OF EQUATORIAL GUINEA

Until 1968, Equatorial Guinea on the west coast of Africa was a Spanish colony and one of its most loyal administrators was Francisco Macías Nguema. In 1961, he travelled to Madrid as spokesperson for a delegation to honour Francisco Franco, Spain's dictator, on the 25th anniversary of his seizure of power.

Son of a witch doctor who claimed magical powers, Francisco was educated in a Catholic school and alienated from the rest of his Fang tribe who had not converted to Christianity. A sickly child, he lived with a lifelong fear of death.

He became a clerk and worked his way up in the Spanish colonial administration, while pocketing bribes. By 1960, he had become deputy president of the Governing Council and a member of the territorial council. It was already feared that he was mentally unstable, possibly because of the use of *bhang*, an edible preparation of cannabis, and *iboga*, a drink with strong hallucinogenic effects. Like Robert Mugabe, he spoke out in favour of Hitler.

Nguema was deputy prime minister in the transitional government and stood against the prime minister at independence to become president. The former prime minister fled for his life, only to be captured and executed.

Equatorial Guinea became a one-party state. Everything in the country fell under his direct rule – including the economy, which he bankrupted. The contents of the coffers of the national bank ended up in his villa, where he spoke to a collection of his victims' heads, while the populace resorted to barter. Slavery was re-introduced. The remaining Spanish colonialists were dispossessed and evacuated. Nigeria pulled out its contract workers. Christianity was banned and the national motto became: 'There is no other God than Macías.'

Increasingly paranoid, he committed mass murder on a whim. Particularly in danger was anyone with an education. Wearing glasses invited a death sentence. In prison, women were raped and men tortured. Boats were destroyed and roads mined in an attempt to prevent people fleeing. Even so, it was estimated that nearly 47 per cent of the people had left the country. Even his wife left. Among those left behind, the death toll was put at anywhere between 20,000 and 80,000.

Eventually, Nguema made the mistake of turning on his own family. After his brother was murdered by the president, Nguema's nephew, Teodoro Obiang Nguema Mbasogo, then head of the National Guard and governor of the notoriously brutal Black Beach prison, along with cousins who had also been to the military academy in Spain, staged a military coup. There was no resistance.

Macías was caught sitting beneath a tree eating sugarcane. $4 million in cash was found in his car while it is said he burnt $100 million belonging to the exchequer in revenge. Tried by a military tribunal, he was sentenced to death 101 times. The sentence had to be carried out by a firing squad made up of the new Moroccan presidential guards as local soldiers feared his inherited magical powers.

## Life and Crimes

**1924** Born 1 January in Spanish Guinea.

**1961** Travels to Madrid to honour Franco.

**1964** Becomes deputy prime minister in transitional government.

**1968** Becomes first president of newly independent Equatorial Guinea.

**1969** 186 suspected dissidents shot, hanged or eaten alive by red ants in national stadium.

**1971** Repeals constitution to give himself dictatorial powers.

**1972** Makes himself president for life; mass arrest of those who voted against him in 1968.

**1973** Aid cut off for cholera epidemic on the island of Pagalu, 100 die; uncooperative statistician dismembered to 'help him learn to count'.

**1975** Newly introduced Equatorial Guinean currency collapses.

**1976** All children 7 to 14 given military training, parents who refuse shot.

**1977** Due to collapse of cocoa production, slavery reintroduced.

**1978** Macías accused of genocide by US.

**1979** Overthrown, tried, condemned and shot.

# Robert Mugabe

◄ 1924–2019 ►

## PRESIDENT OF ZIMBABWE

Robert Mugabe trained to become a teacher in a Catholic missionary school in Rhodesia. He was introduced to nationalist politics at university in South Africa and became a Marxist during the years he spent in Ghana.

On his return to Rhodesia in 1960, he helped form the Zimbabwe African National Union (ZANU) under Ndabaningi Sithole, a group that broke away from Joshua Nkomo's Zimbabwe People's Union on largely tribal lines, and in 1964, he was imprisoned for ten years for political activities. He emerged from prison as ZANU's leader.

With Nkomo he headed the Patriotic Front (PF) while conducting a guerrilla war against Ian Smith's whites-only government from bases in neighbouring Angola, Mozambique and Zambia. In 1979, he joined talks on majority rule in London. In elections the following year, ZANU won a landslide and Mugabe became prime minister.

Despite assurances, Mugabe turned Zimbabwe from a parliamentary democracy to a one-party socialist state with a central committee and a politburo. On 31 December 1987, he became the first executive president of Zimbabwe and first secretary of ZANU–PF. The white middle class began to leave the country and the economy faltered.

In 2000, to shore up his dwindling support, he began expropriating land owned by white farmers and giving it to 'war veterans', who were usually too young to have fought in the war. Much of this land has ended up in the hands of Mugabe's family and cohorts.

After winning a largely discredited election in 2002, Mugabe's regime was subjected to US and EU sanctions, and political opposition, led by Morgan Tsvangirai of the Movement for Democratic Change, intensified, despite intimidation tactics, which included the arrest and beating of Tsvangirai himself in 2007.

In 2008, Mugabe was narrowly defeated by Tsvangirai's MDC in the first round of elections, but a campaign of violence against his supporters led Tsvangirai to pull out of the run-off. However, in a power-sharing

*Mugabe holds forth at a press conference, 1980.*

agreement brokered by South Africa, Mugabe remained president while Tsvangirai became prime minister.

Both parties were anxious to avoid violence in the 2013 elections. Mugabe won, though the elections were not seen to be free and fair. The following year Mugabe fired his vice-president Joice Mujuru, claiming she was plotting against him.

In November 2015, he announced his intention to run for re-election as president in 2018, at the age of 94, and was accepted as the ZANU–PF candidate. However, in November 2017, he sacked another vice-president, Emmerson Mnangagwa, and it was feared that he would name his wife Grace as his successor. Nine days later, Mugabe was put under house arrest by the Zimbabwe National Army.

He was sacked as leader of ZANU-PF and replaced by Mnangagwa. In the face of impeachment, he resigned as president in return for immunity from prosecution for himself and his family, the continuation of the salaries of himself and his wife, and $10 million in cash. He was also allowed to keep the wealth he had amassed, his business interests, his diplomatic status and his house, staff and cars, paid for out of public funds.

Mnangagwa returned from a brief exile to become president. Known as 'The Crocodile', he has been accused of playing a leading role in the massacre of between 20,000 and 30,000 in Matabeleland in the 1980s. Since becoming president, he has been criticized for the violent repression of citizens and the US has imposed sanctions.

Mugabe announced that he would not vote for Mnangawa and ZANU-PF in the 2018 elections. Instead his vote would go to the MDC. Mnangawa won.

Seeking medical help in Singapore, he died there on 6 September 2019. His body was returned to Zimbabwe where he was given a state funeral. Refusing a plot in the Heroes Acre Cemetery in Harare, his family buried him in the courtyard of his family home in his hometown of Kutama.

Meanwhile Mnangawa passed a law threatening critics with the death penalty – it seems one tyrant had simply been replaced by another.

## Life and Crimes

**1924** Born 21 February Kutama, Southern Rhodesia.

**1963** Helps found ZANU.

**1964** Jailed for 'subversive speech'.

**1974** Stages coup to take over ZANU.

**1975** Leaves jail and joins Patriotic Front to oust Ian Smith.

**1979** Lancaster House talks in London end guerrilla war.

**1980** Elected prime minister of Zimbabwe.

**1982** Ousts Nkomo from cabinet, sparking inter-tribal strife.

**1984** Establishes one-party state.

**1987** Becomes executive president.

**1991** Introduces free-market reforms under pressure from the IMF.

**2000** Gives white-owned farm lands to 'war veterans', sparking violence.

**2002** Re-elected president in fixed election.

**2008** Power sharing agreement with MDC.

**2013** Re-elected president in a flawed election.

**2015** Announces he will run again in 2018, aged 94.

**2017** Deposed and forced to resign.

**2019** Dies in Singapore.

# Fidel Castro
## ◄ 1926–2016 ►
## PRESIDENT OF CUBA

Although Cuba's revolutionary leader Fidel Castro honeymooned in the US in 1948 and even considered staying on to study at Columbia University, in the 1960s, he became America's most implacable enemy.

When Fidel Castro came to power in Cuba in 1959, he was not a Communist. Indeed, the US did not hesitate to recognize his regime. He visited Washington, DC, and assured congressmen that he would maintain Cuba's mutual defence treaty with the US, and allow America to keep its naval base at Guantanamo Bay.

However, relations soon cooled when he began nationalizing American-owned sugar plantations. In February 1960, Castro signed a deal to sell sugar to the Soviet Union, a form of trade embargoed by the Americans. In September, he gave a four-hour speech to the United Nations General Assembly in New York, denouncing American 'monopolists' and 'imperialists', and praising the Soviet Union. But it was only in 1961 that Castro's Cuban People's Party – called the Ortodoxos – merged with the Communist Party of Cuba and he became its general secretary. He then began fomenting revolution in Africa and Latin America, and, in 1962, became a threat to the US itself.

Castro was the illegitimate son of a sugar planter from Spain. He was brought up as a Roman Catholic, attending a Jesuit-run boarding school. During his five years at the University of Havana's Law School, he became involved in Cuba's violent brand of student politics. He was accused of the murder of another student leader, although the charge was never proved.

He participated in the attempted invasion of the Dominican Republic in 1947 and the riots in Bogotá, Colombia, the following year. In 1952, he stood as an Ortodoxos candidate for the Cuban House of Representatives. But the former president General Fulgencio Batista seized power and cancelled the elections.

On 26 July 1953, Castro staged an abortive insurrection in Santiago. His comrades were gunned down and he was arrested. At his trial, he

*Fidel Castro in the 1950s.*

attacked the repressive Batista government, concluding with the famous words: 'History will absolve me'.

On release in 1955, he went to Mexico where he formed the revolutionary organization called the 26th of July movement. In December 1956, he returned to Cuba in a small motor cruiser called *Granma*. His small landing force was strafed by Cuban planes, and most of them were killed. Castro survived and, after three years fighting in the Sierra Maestra, rode to power at the head of a popular revolution.

Although Castro called for the US to pledge $30 billion to make Latin America safe for democracy, he soon became authoritarian, first installing himself as Cuban premier, then president, then party chief, forcing the opposition into exile. Within months of taking power, he arrested some 4,500 anti-Castro suspects. They faced mass trials in 1960.

Under President Eisenhower, the CIA began to train anti-Castro Cuban exiles. Castro's response was to seize all US assets in Cuba, including the American embassy. Although President Kennedy imposed an embargo on Cuban goods, many Europeans saw Castro as a romantic figure: Britain became the first nation to break the US blockade.

US antipathy to Castro resulted in the unsuccessful invasion at the Bay of Pigs. Castro responded by allowing the Soviets to install nuclear missiles on the island, precipitating the Cuban Missile Crisis.

After the failure of the Bay of Pigs invasion, the CIA tried unsuccessfully to assassinate him and employed a 'dirty tricks' division who dreamed up such ideas as poisoning his cigars and sprinkling depilatory powder in his diving mask. The idea behind this last wacky scheme was that if Fidel lost his famous beard, with it would go his support. One attempt involving a poisoned chocolate milkshake failed when the agent responsible for planting it put it in the freezer by mistake, resulting in Castro being unable to drink it. Rogue CIA agents even tried to involve the Mafia, who had lost their casinos in Havana.

Castro had a well-known weakness for women. One of his lovers was a young German woman named Marita Lorenz who lived in New York. After their affair was over, the CIA persuaded her to return to Havana to poison him. According to Marita, he knew she had come to kill him and handed her his revolver, but she could not pull the trigger.

Lee Harvey Oswald, Jack Ruby and others involved in the assassination of President Kennedy were closely involved with dissident Cubans, as were the 'plumbers' who burgled the Democratic Nation Committee offices in the Watergate building in 1972.

Despite assassination attempts and international isolation – especially after the collapse of the Soviet Union – Castro clung on to power. Meanwhile his people risked almost anything to flee, and the country continued to decay. In 2003 seventy-five dissidents were jailed for up to twenty-eight years for daring to speak out against the regime. It was reported they had concrete slabs for a bed, ate food that would 'make a pig vomit' and used lavatories that 'regurgitate their fetid contents around the clock'. On the other hand, the Cuba people enjoyed an efficient and generous welfare state and health system.

In July 2006 Castro temporarily handed power to his brother, Raul, before undergoing surgery. Two years later, he gave up the presidency permanently, and in 2011 he resigned as leader of the Communist Party. He continued a behind-the-scenes role in foreign affairs, meeting foreign leaders – even the Pope when he visited Cuba in 2012, but refusing to meet Barrack Obama when he visited in 2015.

China awarded him the Confucius Peace Prize and, at the age of 90, he continued making speeches urging Cubans to retain their communist ideals. He died on 25 November 2016. After nine days' mourning, his funeral procession reversed the route on which he had come to power as a guerrilla, making the 560-mile trip from Havana to Santiago de Cuba where he was buried.

# Life and Crimes

**1926** Born 13 August near Birán, Cuba.

**1947** Joins abortive attempt by Dominican exiles to overthrow the regime of Generalissimo Rafael Trujillo.

**1948** Takes part in riots in Bogotá, Colombia.

**1950** Joins the Cuban People's Party – the Ortodoxos.

**1952** Becomes candidate for House of Representatives, but the elections are cancelled due to Batista's coup.

**1953** Leads suicidal attack on barracks in Santiago de Cuba and is arrested.

**1955** Released in an amnesty, flees to Mexico.

**1956** Lands in Cuba with small band of guerrillas.

**1959** Overthrows Batista government and takes power.

**1960** Begins mass show trials.

**1961** Repels CIA-backed invasion at Bay of Pigs.

**1962** Cuban Missile Crisis threatens nuclear war.

**1964** Begins attempt to 'export revolution'.

**1975** Sends troops to Angola.

**1978** Sends troops to Ethiopia.

**1980** Emerges as leader of non-aligned world, despite obvious Soviet backing.

**1991** Collapse of Soviet Union forces Castro to open doors to tourism and introduce a dollar economy – revising the policy of the previous 30 years.

**2008** Retires as president.

**2011** Resigns as leader of Communist Party.

**2015** Meets Pope Benedict XVI, despite his opposition to the Cuban government.

**2016** Dies on 25 November; buried in Santa Ifigenia Cemetery, Santiago de Cuba.

# Efrain Ríos Montt
## ◄ 1926–2018 ►
## DICTATOR OF GUATEMALA

The murderous dictator General Efrain Ríos Montt is, like many of his Latin American peers, a product of the School of the Americas run by the US military in Panama. From the 1950s onwards the notorious 'coup school' taught its students how to contribute to the defeat of communism – and further US interests – by usurping political power in Latin America by any means necessary, including torture, assassination and 'disappearance'. Ríos Montt is also an ordained minister of the authoritarian, right-wing Gospel Outreach evangelical Church, based in California, which has been expanding fast in the South American region.

After a US-orchestrated military coup in 1954, Guatemala became a key component of US 'counter-insurgency' strategy in Central America. However, in 1960 a civil war broke out which has continued unabated ever since. The situation worsened in 1970 when the presidential election was won by the 'law and order' candidate Arana Osorio, who promised to 'pacify' the country by exterminating 'habitual criminals' and leftist guerrillas. In practice, this meant death squads linked to the police or military began the organized murder of opposition leaders.

In 1974 Ríos Montt stood as leader of the progressive wing of the armed forces. When it became clear that he had won the election, counting was suspended and his opponent General Kjell Laugerud García was declared the winner.

In March 1982, the elections were won by a coalition candidate, General Angel Aríbal Guevara. But on 23 March, a junta headed by Ríos Montt seized power. He quickly dissolved the junta and took absolute power, pledging to disband the death squads, clean up corruption and end the guerrilla war by launching the so-called 'guns and beans' offensive against Guatemala's insurgents. A subsequent report commissioned by the UN found that at least 448 villages – mostly Indian – had been wiped off the map. The targeting of the Mayan peoples forced hundreds of thousands to flee to the mountains or to neighbouring Mexico. Many of those who remained were corralled into 'hamlets' to produce cash crops for export.

According to Amnesty International, in just four months there were more than 2,000 fully documented extrajudicial killings by the Guatemalan army: 'People of all ages were not only shot, they were burned alive, hacked to death, disembowelled, drowned, beheaded. Small children were smashed against rocks or bayoneted to death.' However, US President Ronald Reagan, who visited Guatemala at the time, hailed Ríos Montt as 'totally dedicated to democracy'.

'We do not have a policy of scorched earth. We have a policy of scorched Communists,' Ríos Montt added.

Soon he became an international embarrassment. He was overthrown in August 1983 by General Oscar Humberto Mejía Victores, who returned the country to democracy.

But this did not remove Ríos Montt from power completely, far from it. The political party he founded, the ultra-right-wing Guatemalan Republican Alliance (FRG), expanded rapidly and gained control of a majority in Congress. The current President of Guatemala, Alfonso Portillo – a former guerrilla – is a Ríos Montt protégé.

Although Ríos Montt was actually president of the Congress, he was forbidden from running for president of the country by a constitutional law prohibiting former dictators from running for office.

However, he succeeded in getting the Supreme Court to overturn that ruling after inciting thousands of FRG supporters to cause havoc in Guatemala City, on a day that became known as 'jueves negro' (black Thursday).

The electorate, however, stood firm and he gained just 11 per cent of the votes, well behind the victorious Óscar Berger of the Grand National Alliance.

Meanwhile, Ríos Montt's human rights record was threatening to come home to roost. His own brother, Bishop Mario Ríos Montt, who succeeded the assassinated Bishop Juan Gerardi as head of the Catholic Church's human rights office in Guatemala in 1998, promised to continue Gerardi's work, uncovering the truth behind the massacre of 200,000 people during the civil war and the genocide of the Mayan people during his brother's presidency in 1982–83.

In 1999, Nobel Peace Prize-winner Rigoberta Menchú brought a human rights case against Ríos Montt and the campaign to bring him to justice gathered momentum.

In 2006, a Spanish court issued an international arrest warrant, but Ríos Montt continued to seek political power at home. In 2007 he ran for Congress and won a seat, leading the FRG delegation once again and, more significantly, rendering him immune from prosecution.

However, in January 2012 his term in office expired and he was brought before the Guatemalan court, where he was charged with genocide and crimes against humanity, making him the first former head of state to be tried for genocide in his own country. The following year he was sentenced to 80 years, but the sentence was quashed by the Constitutional Court. A retrial was underway when he died on 1 April 2018.

## Life and Crimes

**1926**  Born 16 June in Huehuetenango.
**1950s**  Attends 'coup school' in Panama.
**1974**  Wins election but is denied presidency.
**1982**  Stages coup, begins genocide of Mayans.
**1983**  Ousted from office.
**1998**  Brother appointed to investigate 'disappearances'.
**2003**  Stands for presidency again.
**2006**  International arrest warrant issued against him.
**2007**  Regains a seat in Congress.
**2012**  Placed under house arrest.
**2013**  Sentenced to 80 years, but sentence overturned.
**2018**  Dies during retrial.

# Pol Pot
## ◄ 1925–1998 ►
## LEADER OF CAMBODIA

Pol Pot was responsible for the deaths of over a million of his countrymen in a bloodthirsty experiment to create a moneyless socialist society and turn the clock back in Cambodia to 'Year Zero'.

Born Saloth Sâr, Pol Pot worked on a rubber plantation in his youth and spent two years studying to become a Buddhist monk. During World War II, he joined the resistance movement of Ho Chi Minh, which went on to fight the colonialist French. By 1946, he was a member of the underground Indochinese Communist Party. In 1949, he won a scholarship to study radio electronics in Paris, but he spent his time there involved in political activities, failing his exams three years in a row, a failure later seen as contributing to his anti-intellectualism. Returning to Cambodia, he worked as a geography teacher in a private school in the capital Phnom Penh and wrote articles for left-wing publications.

When the French withdrew from Indochina in 1954, Prince Norodom Sihanouk took power in Cambodia. Pol Pot opposed him. At the founding congress of the Cambodian Communist Party in 1960, he was elected to the central committee, becoming party secretary in 1963.

Fearing Sihanouk's repression, Pol Pot and other Communist leaders fled to the jungle. There he took command of a guerrilla army dismissed by Sihanouk as the Khmer Rouge – the Red Cambodians. Although Sihanouk maintained a strict neutrality, the war in neighbouring Vietnam was destabilizing Cambodia. In 1970, the United States backed the overthrow of Sihanouk's regime by the pro-American General Lon Nol. With the backing of the Vietnamese Communists, who had established camps in the border area, the Khmer Rouge waged a guerrilla war against Lon Nol. The US incursion into Cambodia in 1970 and its continuing cross-border bombing campaign served to swell the Khmer Rouge's numbers and gain international sympathy for its cause.

In 1975, as South Vietnam was falling to the Communists, the Khmer Rouge overthrew the US-backed regime in Cambodia. Pol Pot changed the country's name to Kampuchea. He evacuated Phnom Penh, marching its two million inhabitants out into the countryside at gunpoint. His aim was to turn the educated middle-class city-dwellers into the virtuous hard-working peasants who had supported his guerrilla army during its years of struggle.

His plan was to turn Cambodia back to 'Year Zero' and build a perfect socialist society from the bottom up. Money and property were abolished. Books were burnt. Private houses were demolished, temples desecrated and every symbol of Western technology – from cars to medical equipment – was destroyed.

To make his utopian society, Pol Pot transformed Cambodia into one vast slave-labour camp. Children were encouraged to inform on their parents and family life was all but extinguished. All professional people – including doctors and teachers – were killed, along with anyone who spoke French or wore glasses, which was considered the mark of an intellectual. Their children were buried alive. Schools were closed, except for those devoted to political indoctrination, and everyone above the age of five was expected to work in the fields or factories sixteen hours a day. Those who could not meet production quotas or complained were killed on the spot. During the four years of Pol Pot's rule, around 1.7 million people – over 20 per cent of the population – died as a result of disease, starvation, maltreatment, forced labour, torture and execution.

In 1979, the Vietnamese invaded and put an end to the holocaust. Pol Pot fled with his followers to the hill country on the Thai border where they continued the struggle with the backing of the US, Chinese and British governments. International condemnation and sanctions, led by a United States still embittered at the way their war in Vietnam had turned out, eventually forced the Vietnamese to withdraw and the Khmer Rouge returned to power in various coalition governments, while Pol Pot continued his murderous ways in the countryside. Eventually even the Communists disowned him, albeit half-heartedly. Pol Pot never stood trial for his many crimes, and he died of natural causes aged 72.

# Life and Crimes

**1925**  Born Saloth Sâr 19 May in Kompong Thom province, Cambodia.

**1946**  Joins Cambodian Communist Party.

**1954**  Becomes a teacher.

**1963**  Flees the capital; takes to the jungle.

**1975**  Overthrows US-backed government; declares Year Zero.

**1979**  Vietnam invasion ousts Khmer Rouge.

**1982**  Khmer Rouge joins coalition government.

**1985**  Retires.

**1998**  Dies 15 April in Cambodian jungle.

# Mobutu Sese Seko

### ◄ 1930–1997 ►

## DICTATOR OF THE CONGO

Born Joseph-Désiré Mobutu, he joined the Belgian Congolese Army in 1949, rising to the rank of sergeant-major – the highest rank Africans were allowed to attain – before turning to journalism in 1956.

He joined the Congolese National Movement (MNC) in 1958, representing them at talks on independence in Brussels. When the Congo won its independence in June 1960, he became defence secretary. In September of the same year, he staged a coup during which the popular leader Patrice Lumumba was killed.

Although in February 1961 he handed power back to President Joseph Kasavubu, staying on as commander in chief of the army, in 1965 he staged another coup, this time holding on to the presidency himself. He ruled by decree and the Movement for the Revolution, which he headed, became the only party permitted.

He nationalized the copper mines in Katanga and Africanized names throughout the country. In October 1971, he changed the nation's name to the Republic of Zaire. The following January he took the name Mobutu Sese Seko Koko Ngbendu Wa Za Banga – which means 'the all-powerful warrior who, because of his endurance and inflexible will to win, will go from conquest to conquest, leaving a wake of fire'.

*Mobutu with Katangan prisoners on live television during the Katangan unrest in Zaire, 1977.*

Re-elected to the presidency in 1970 and 1977, he looted the country, amassing one of the world's largest fortunes abroad. As a result inflation soared to 6,000 per cent a year. The army was on the point of rebelling when he issued a five-million-zaire banknote to pay them. Officially these were worth $2, but shopkeepers refused to take them, provoking the army to go on a killing spree that resulted in 300 deaths.

With the end of the Cold War, Mobutu lost Western support for his government, but he managed to hold on to power until, in 1997, friendless and ill, he was ousted by rebel leader Laurent Kabila and went into exile, first in Togo, then Morocco, where he died of prostate cancer in September that year.

## Life and Crimes

**1930**  Born 14 October in Lisala, Belgian Congo.

**1949**  Joins Belgian Congolese Army.

**1956**  Leaves army to become journalist.

**1958**  Joins Congolese National Movement.

**1960**  Represents MNC at independence talks; becomes defence secretary in new government; stages first coup.

**1961**  Returns power to president; stays on as commander in chief.

**1965**  Stages second coup; becomes president.

**1971**  Changes name of country to Zaire.

**1972**  Changes own name to Mobutu Sese Seko Koko Ngbendu Wa Za Banga.

**1993**  Army on point of rebellion for not being paid; agrees to hold democratic elections but continues to stall.

**1997**  Ousted by Laurent Kabila; dies 7 September in Rabat, Morocco.

# Mengistu Haile Mariam

◄ Born 1937 ►

## RULER OF ETHIOPIA

An Ethiopian army officer, Mengistu was trained in the United States. Rising to the rank of major, he plotted a coup, deposing the Emperor Haile Selassie in September 1974. Selassie was held under house arrest in his palace until he was strangled on Mengistu's orders the following year.

On 23 November Mengistu ordered the assassination of the moderate chairman of the country's ruling Provisional Military Administrative Council (PMAC) and urged the killing of 60 leaders of the imperial regime.

In February 1977, now promoted to lieutenant colonel, Mengistu had the new chairman killed, making himself head of state. He then unleashed the 'Red Terror' campaign to crush any resistance and, with Cuban soldiers

*Mengistu and his advisers during a parade in Addis Ababa, 1975.*

and Soviet arms, he repelled the Somalian invasion of the Somali-speaking Ogden.

In 1984, he established the Ethopian Workers' Party. He drafted a new constitution and was elected president by a new national assembly. By this time Eritrea and Tigray in the north had rebelled. And when Soviet backing ended, he fled to Zimbabwe, where his fellow dictator Robert Mugabe still shelters him. In January 2007 he was sentenced to life imprisonment in Ethiopia, having been found guilty in absentia of genocide. This sentence was amended to the death penalty following an unsuccessful appeal in 2008. However, the Zimbabwe government refused to give him up.

## Life and Crimes

**1937** Born in Kefa province, Ethiopia.

**1974** Heads plot to overthrow the emperor; assassinates political rivals.

**1975** Haile Selassie strangled on his orders.

**1977** Murders other members of government; makes himself head of state; unleashes 'Red Terror' campaign.

**1986** Drafts new constitution.

**1987** Elected president under its provisions.

**1991** Flees to Zimbabwe.

**2001** Given leave to stay permanently.

**2007** Found guilty of genocide.

# Saddam Hussein

## ◄ 1937–2006 ►

## PRESIDENT OF IRAQ

Born Saddam Al-Tikriti and orphaned at nine, he was raised by his uncle Khairallah Talfah who led an unsuccessful Nazi-backed coup in 1941. A slow learner, Saddam was refused entry into the Baghdad Military Academy. Instead he joined the Ba'ath Socialist Party in 1957.

Having already killed a Communist politician who had stood against his uncle, Saddam volunteered to assassinate President Adbul Karim Kassim who had overthrown the Iraqi monarchy in 1958. The attempt failed and Saddam, wounded in the leg, fled to Egypt, dropping the name Al-Tikriti and using his father's first name, Hussein, as his last to avoid arrest.

He returned to Baghdad, where he organized the Ba'athist militia, who seized power in 1963. Later that year, the Ba'athists were ousted and Saddam was imprisoned, but he escaped and, as leader of the Ba'athist party, staged another coup in 1968. At first he ruled jointly with President Ahmad Hassam al-Bakr, who stood aside in 1979. Saddam then consolidated his position as head of state by putting to death hundreds of rivals.

Saddam and his family took hold of all the levers of power. He instigated a cult of personality in an effort to make himself leader of the Arab world and using his secret police, eliminated any opposition. Asked by a European interviewer about reports that the Baghdad authorities might have tortured and killed opponents of the regime, Saddam replied: 'Of course, what do you expect if they oppose the regime?'

In 1980, he invaded the Iranian oilfields, but the offensive bogged down into a costly war of attrition, ending with a stalemate in 1988. Hundreds of thousands had been killed. That same year, he used nerve gas against the Kurds who opposed his rule.

In 1990, he invaded Kuwait. The following year a US-led coalition drove his forces out of Kuwait, inflicting a crushing defeat, but leaving him in power. During the war, Saddam authorized missile attacks on Israel, a non-combatant. His forces terrorized the populace of Kuwait and while withdrawing, polluted the Persian Gulf with oil spills and set fire to over 300 oil wells. Putting down a resulting rebellion of Shi'ia in the south of Iraq he razed towns and drained their marshland home.

Twelve years of United Nations sanctions failed to remove him from power and in 2003 Anglo-American forces invaded Iraq. Saddam disappeared, but his two sons Uday and Qusay, both psychopathic killers, died in a gun battle. Mass graves soon came to light: it seems that Saddam's executioners were still killing hundreds of enemies of the regime even as American tanks were rolling into Baghdad.

On 15 December 2003, soldiers from the US 4th Infantry Division, acting on intelligence received over the eight months since they had been

*Modern bogeyman Saddam Hussein, strongman of Iraq.*

in country, mounted a dawn attack on a small Iraqi town named Ad-Dawr. The town is located approximately ten miles south of Saddam's home town of Tikrit. During the raid, they discovered an underground bunker. Crouched in the bunker, dishevelled, unshaven and unwashed, was the former Iraqi 'strongman', the leader of his people and father of his country. Unlike his sons, Hussein Snr chose surrender without a fight as the better part of valour.

Tried by the Iraqi Special Tribunal for the 1982 murder of 148 Shi'ites in Dujail, he was found guilty of crimes against humanity and sentenced to hang. Footage of him being led to his death on 30 December 2006 was broadcast around the world.

# Life and Crimes

**1937**  Born 28 April in Tikrit, Iraq.

**1957**  Joins Ba'ath Party.

**1960**  Makes unsuccessful assassination attempt on Iraqi president; escapes to Egypt.

**1962–1963**  Studies at Cairo Law School.

**1963**  Leads Ba'ath militia in coup; ousted from power and imprisoned.

**1968**  New coup brings Ba'athists and Saddam back to power.

**1979**  Takes over as president; murders hundreds of rivals.

**1980**  Invades Iran.

**1988**  Gases the Kurds.

**1990**  Invades Kuwait.

**1991**  Kicked out of Kuwait; drains the homeland of the Marsh Arabs.

**2003**  Ousted from power by Anglo-American invasion.

**2003**  Captured hiding in a hole by US troops.

**2006**  Found guilty of crimes against humanity and executed on 30 December.

# Slobodan Milošević

◀ 1941–2006 ▶

## PRESIDENT OF SERBIA

Slobodan Milošević was the Serbian leader during the break-up of Yugoslavia. He plunged his people into war and his ruthless pursuit of 'ethnic cleansing' led to numerous massacres, until finally NATO intervened to defend the people of Kosovo. Milošević was then overthrown by his own people and was eventually handed over to the UN War Crimes Tribunal in The Hague.

Milošević was an obscure Communist Party apparatchik until April 1987, when he made a speech to a crowd of angry Serbs in Pristina, capital of Kosovo, who were protesting against alleged harassment by the majority Albanian community. He said famously that no one would ever be allowed to beat them, a statement of defiance which would become a rallying cry for Serb nationalists.

He wrested control of the Serbian Communist Party from his friend and ally Ivan Stambolic and, in 1989, he became President of Serbia. The following January the Yugoslav Communist Party fell apart when the Slovenian and Croatian delegations walked out of the party congress in Belgrade, leading to the break-up of the party.

In July, the Serbian Communist Party changed its name to the Serbian Socialist Party, but it retained its assets, power structures and control of the state media. Milošević warned that if the Yugoslav nation dissolved, it would be necessary to redraw Serbia's boundaries to include Serbs living in other republics.

When Croatia declared independence, the Serb minority who had proclaimed regional autonomy in Krajina looked to Milošević for support – and got it. By December 1991, the army and Serbian separatists had taken nearly a third of Croatia's territory, including Krajina and most of eastern and western Slavonia. Some 20,000 people were killed, and a further 400,000 made homeless. The UN imposed economic sanctions.

Bosnia declared independence in April 1992 and violence broke out throughout the republic, with Milošević vowing to defend the Serbian minority there as well as protecting them from what he called 'Croatian genocide' and 'Islamic fundamentalism'. More than three years of war followed, the bloodiest in Europe since World War II. Serbian war crimes, including, shamefully, massacres within the so-called 'UN safe areas' of Gorazde and Srebrenica, came to public attention and Serbia was further isolated as a pariah state.

In 1995, Croatia recovered much of the territory earlier captured by the Serbs, resulting in the exodus of some 200,000 Serbs from their self-proclaimed Republic of Serbian Krajina. This was followed by a successful offensive against Bosnian Serbs in Bosnia. Three weeks of NATO bombing forced Milošević to the bargaining table and the Dayton Peace Agreement ended the war in Bosnia.

The war had made Milošević unpopular, but he rode out massive waves of protests against his government during the winter of 1996–97, when tens of thousands of people took to the streets, contesting the results of municipal elections. Many demonstrators were brutally beaten by the Serbian police. After three months of protests, Milošević caved in, conceding stolen municipal elections to the opposition. But in July 1997 Milošević was elected president of Yugoslavia by the lame-duck federal parliament, which was controlled by his supporters.

He then tried to drive the Muslim majority out of Kosovo. NATO began its bombing campaign, and there was a feeling of disbelief among many Yugoslavs. But Milošević rode out the storm, and for a while consolidated support as Serbs united against the West.

The NATO bombing campaign left Serbia in ruins. Milošević finally withdrew his troops from Kosovo. With Serbia's infrastructure ruined and its economy crippled by new sanctions, Milošević remodelled himself as the rebuilder of the nation. However, in 2000 he was forced to call elections.

When Milošević refused to recognize the election victory of opposition leader Vojislav Kostunica, hundreds of thousands of people took to the streets and a national strike was declared. The Serbian Orthodox Church and parts of the state media withdrew their support. Ten days after the election, protesters stormed parliament and the state TV station, setting them alight. Many policemen took off their helmets and joined the protesters.

On 6 October Milošević was forced to concede defeat. The following day Kostunica was sworn in as the new Yugoslav president. In June 2001

Milošević was handed over to The Hague tribunal for trial, but died of a heart attack in March 2006, before the trial ended.

# Life and Crimes

**1941**  Born 29 August in Pozarevac, Yugoslavia.

**1963**  Joins Yugoslav Communist Party.

**1987**  Speech in Pristina brings him to national attention.

**1988**  Installs followers in power in autonomous provinces, including Kosovo.

**1989**  Ousts Ivan Stambolic to take over as President of Serbia.

**1990**  Alters constitution to take direct power of autonomous provinces.

**1991**  Backs Serbians in fighting in Croatia, taking almost a third of Croatia; Serb leaders in Bosnia proclaim separate state.

**1992**  War breaks out in Bosnia.

**1995**  Croatian forces recover Serb-held territory; 200,000 Serbs flee; NATO air strikes force Milošević to accept Dayton Peace Agreement.

**1996**  Anti-Milošević protests brutally suppressed.

**1997**  Becomes Yugoslav president.

**1998**  Milošević rejects calls for end to ethnic cleansing in Kosovo.

**1999**  NATO planes bomb Serbia; Serbs withdraw from Kosovo.

**2000**  Vojislav Kostunica wins election; strikes and civil disobedience force Milošević to step down.

**2001**  Sent by the Serbian government to The Hague to face trial.

**2002**  Trial begins.

**2006**  Dies of a heart attack.

# Muammar al-Gaddafi
◄ 1942–2011 ►

## PRESIDENT OF LIBYA

Born a Bedouin in the desert, Muammar al-Gaddafi was reared in the tradition of fighting imperialism. His grandfather had been killed by an Italian colonist in 1911. However, he showed no gratitude to the British who expelled the Italians from his native Libya in World War II: to Gaddafi, all Europeans were alike.

From an early age he idolized Gamal Abdel Nasser, the Egyptian soldier who seized power in Egypt in a coup in 1954 and nationalized the Suez Canal. As a child, he would tune into Radio Cairo and, at the age of 16, Gaddifi began his own revolutionary cell which plotted the overthrow of King Idris of Libya, even though the king had turned his back on his former allies, the British, and joined the Arab League.

In 1959, oil was discovered in Libya, which brought wealth to the country, but also brought more foreigners in the shape of the oil companies. At the University of Libya, Gaddafi read history and political science. Initially he was a Marxist, but then rejected communism in favour of Islam. At university he became known as a troublemaker for his fierce condemnation of Israel and Zionism.

Realizing that Nasser had come to power via the army, Gaddafi enrolled in the Libyan Military Academy in Benghazi when he graduated from university in 1964, and here he and his friends continued to plot the overthrow of the Libyan government.

After he graduated from the academy in 1965, he spent a year in England at signals school. He also studied armoured warfare there. On his return he was promoted to Adjutant of the Signals Corps.

In 1969, Gaddafi and his young friends pre-empted senior officers who were plotting against the king and staged a bloodless coup of their own. They seized the Royal Palace, government offices, the radio and TV stations, and the newspapers. Gaddafi was just 27 years old.

However, some of the conspirators wanted to maintain ties with the West, so Gaddafi asked Nasser for help. With the aid of Nasser's troops, Gaddafi made sure that his anti-Western line prevailed. British and American bases were closed and, in 1970, Jews and Italians were expelled.

Gaddafi tried to implement Nasser's brand of socialism, nationalizing the oil companies and starting rapid industrialization, which failed. He also tried to export revolution and was implicated in attempted coups in the Sudan and Egypt, and he interfered in the long-running civil war in Chad.

Banning alcohol and gambling in accordance with Islamic principles, he began a cult of personality and outlined his vision of Islamic socialism in two volumes of *The Green Book*, published in 1976 and 1980. His regime backed a number of revolutionary or terrorist groups including the Provisional IRA in Northern Ireland, and the Black Panthers and the Nation of Islam in the US, and Carlos 'the Jackal'. Émigré opponents were assassinated by his agents who also backed terrorist outrages in Europe perpetrated by Palestinian or other Arab extremists. He is thought to have financed the Black September Movement, responsible for the kidnapping of Israeli athletes at the 1972 Munich Olympics, and the bombing of a German discotheque in 1986, which killed one American and one German woman and wounded 150, including 44 Americans. In retaliation, US warplanes based in the UK bombed Libya in 1986, killing or wounding several of his children and narrowly missing Gaddafi himself. When Pan Am Flight 103 was blown up over the Scottish town of Lockerbie in 1988, suspicion eventually fell on Gadaffi's Libya, and in 2001 a Libyan government official was found guilty of the bombing. Libya admitted responsibility in 2003, and agreed a compensation package to be paid to relatives of the victims. In February 2011, the Arab Spring uprisings in Tunisia and Egypt spread into Libya, triggering a civil war in which Gadaffi showed no regard for the welfare of his people. The International Criminal Court issued an arrest warrant against him for crimes against humanity and, though he was eventually captured alive after the fall of his last stronghold, Sirte, in October he was killed by fighters from the Libyan National Liberation Army before he could come to trial.

# Life and Crimes

**1942** Born near Surt, Libya.

**1964** Enrols in Military Academy.

**1965** Graduates and is sent to signals school in England.

**1966** Commissioned as a signals officer.

**1969** Deposes King Idris I and takes power; ousts co-conspirators with help of Egyptian troops.

**1970** Closes British and US bases; expels Jews and Italians.

**1973** Nationalizes oil companies.

**1974** Espouses 'Islamic socialism'.

**1976** Publishes part one of *The Green Book*.

**1980** Publishes part two of *The Green Book*.

**1986** US bombs Libya in retaliation for Gaddafi's support of terrorism.

**1988** Liberalizes economic policies after his ideological doctrines are seen to fail.

**1988** Libya accused of bombing of Pan Am Flight 103: US-inspired sanctions put in place.

**2003** Libya admits responsibility for Pan Am bomb, and agrees compensation for the victims.

**2011** Ousted from power and killed during the Libyan civil war.

# Hissène Habré

## ◄ 1942–2021 ►

## DICTATOR OF CHAD

Born in 1942 in the Boukou district of Chad, Hissène Habré was educated in Paris. He returned to Chad in 1971, but left for Tripoli the following year where he established a guerrilla army called the Armed Forces of the North (FAN).

Moving across the border into northern Chad, Habré's army funded itself by extortion and ransoming kidnapped Europeans. In 1980, President Goukouni Oueddei requested the support of Libya in the continuing struggle between the Christian/black southern region and the Arab/Muslim north, forcing Habré to withdraw to the Sudan. However, he soon reoccupied towns in eastern Chad.

When the peacekeeping forces of the Organization of African Unity withdrew in 1982, Habré seized power, but an opposition government under Goukouni Oueddei was formed with Libyan backing. A full-scale civil war broke out in 1983, which Habré won with French backing. When France withdrew its troops in 1984, Libya pushed deeper into Chad in 1986. With French and US support, Habré pushed the forces of Muammar al-Gaddafi out of the country and began to make incursions into Libya. A truce was called in 1987, but in April 1989 Habré faced an unsuccessful coup attempt by the interior minister, Brahim Mahamot Itno, with military advisers, Hassan Djamouss and Idriss Déby. Itno was arrested and Djamouss was killed, but Déby escaped and began new attacks the following year. By late 1990 his Movement for Chadian National Salvation forces had captured Abéché in eastern Chad, and on 1 December Habré fled to Cameroon, then to Senegal. Déby formed a new government with himself as president.

A commission set up in 1991 accused Habré's administration of 40,000 political murders and 200,000 cases of torture. Human rights groups say they have detailed 97 cases of political killings, 142 cases of torture and 100 'disappearances'. The United Nations backed his prosecution for human rights violations, but Senegal has repeatedly blocked attempts to extradite him.

However, in 2016, he faced trial by an international tribunal set up by the African Union in Senegal, the first former head of state to be prosecuted for crimes against humanity in the courts of another nation. Convicted, he was sentenced to life imprisonment. He died on 24 August 2021 after testing positive for COVID-19.

# Life and Crimes

**1942** Born in Boukou, Chad.

**1971** Returns to Chad after education in France.

**1972** Forms guerrilla army in Tripoli.

**1980** Forced to withdraw to the Sudan due to Libyan intervention.

**1982** Seizes power.

**1983–1984** Civil war breaks out; Habré wins with French backing.

**1986** Libya invades northern Chad; Habré ousts Libyans with French and US support.

**1987** Truce called.

**1989** Foils coup.

**1990** Ousted by Idriss Déby; flees to Senegal.

**1991** Commission accuses Habré of 40,000 murders and 200,000 cases of torture.

**2016** Tried by the Extraordinary African Chambers in Senegal; sentenced to life.

**2021** Dies of COVID-19.

# Sani Abacha
## ◄ 1943–1998 ►
### DICTATOR OF NIGERIA

Leader of the last successful military coup d'état in Nigeria, Sani Abacha had worked his way to the top, being the first full military general to reach that position without missing a rank on the way and he had been involved in the previous seven coups and coup attempts.

Born in 1943, he was commissioned in 1963 after attending the Mons Officer Cadet School in Aldershot. In 1969, he fought in the Nigerian Civil War when the state of Biafra tried to secede from the federation.

In 1983, he was appointed a member of the Supreme Military Council and played a prominent role in the coup d'état that put General Muhammadu Buhari in power that year. Two years later Buhari was ousted by the SMC who put General Ibrahim Babangida in his place. Abacha was named Army Chief of Staff. Three years after that he became Minister of Defence.

After six years in power Babangida sought to return Nigeria to civilian rule, but when he annulled the results of the presidential election in 1993, citing irregularities, Abacha seized power, ruling as Head of State and Commander-in-Chief. He issued a decree putting his government beyond the jurisdiction of the courts, effectively giving him absolute power.

Opposition newspapers were banned and he was given the right to detain anyone for up to three months without trial. The presumed winner of the 1993 election businessman Moshood Abiola died in jail on charges of treason and the 1979 constitution was suspended.

Abacha's Chief Security Officer Hamza al-Mustapha ran a vast network of spies and informants, while Abacha himself assembled a personal security force of 3,000 men trained in North Korea. The Nigeria Police Force was retrained and human rights abuses were widespread.

Writer Ken Saro-Wiwa and others were executed for opposing Royal Dutch Shell drilling for oil in the Ogoni region. Wole Soyinka, winner of the 1986 Nobel Prize for Literature, was charged *in absentia* with treason.

But the oil brought prosperity. Inflation fell, along with the national debt. This allowed Abacha and his clique to siphon money offshore. An estimated $1.4 billion disappeared this way. Abacha also buddied up with Colonel Gaddafi and intervened in the Liberian Civil War.

Early in 1998, he claimed he was going to return Nigeria to civilian government, but he had no intention of relinquishing power. He coerced the country's five political parties into endorsing him as sole presidential candidate. However, before the election he died suddenly at the age of 55. It is thought that he was assassinated.

## Life and Crimes

**1943** Born in Kano, Nigeria.

**1963** Receives military training in the UK.

**1969** Fights in the Nigerian Civil War against the Biafrans.

**1983** Appointed to the Supreme Military Council after aiding the coup which toppled President Shehu Shagari.

**1985** Named Army Chief of Staff by Ibrahim Babangida.

**1988** Becomes Minister of Defence.

**1993** Orchestrates a coup and places himself as head of state.

**1998** Shortly before the election, he dies in mysterious circumstances.

# Omar al-Bashir

◀ Born 1944 ▶

## DICTATOR OF SUDAN

In March 2009, Omar al-Bashir earned the distinction of being the first sitting head of state to be indicted by the International Criminal Court in The Hague. An arrest warrant was issued for war crimes and crimes against humanity over the conduct of the fighting in the breakaway state of Dafur. Later charges of genocide were added. But first he had to complete his sentence in Sudan for corruption and money laundering.

Of Bedouin descent, he was born in the small city of Shendi on the bank of the Nile in northern Sudan. Educated in Khartoum, he joined the army. From 1975 to 1981, he served as military attaché to the United Arab Emirates. Returning home, he took command of an armoured parachute brigade, then an infantry brigade.

From 1983 a civil war was raging, resulting in famine. In 1989, the army presented an ultimatum to the democratically elected Prime Minister Sadiq al-Mahdi, telling him to either end the war or give them the means to do so. He responded by trying to arrest those he believed were plotting to oust him. In response, Bashir led a band of military officers who removed Mahdi in a bloodless coup. Bashir became head of state, prime minister, defence minister and commander-in-chief of the armed forces.

Political parties were banned and sharia law was imposed nationwide, affronting Christians in the south. Punishments included amputations and stoning. The army was purged. Newspapers were closed and politicians and journalists jailed. Bashir then made himself president.

After three years in office, he ran a presidential election in which he was the only candidate allowed to stand. He wrote a new constitution and when he faced limited opposition in the National Assembly he sent troops and tanks to oust the speaker, his friend and mentor Hassan al-Turabi, the leader of the National Islamic Front who had invited Osama bin Laden to move to Sudan in 1991.

Bashir was re-elected in 2000, though the main opposition parties boycotted the election, accusing the government of vote rigging. However, he did succeed in ending the civil war with a peace agreement in 2005, giving the south autonomy for six years until a referendum in 2011 gave South Sudan its independence.

But in 2003 war had broken out in the western region of Darfur where non-Arabs complained that the government was favouring Arabs over them. The army, police and Janjaweed militia responded with a campaign of ethnic cleansing against the non Arabs, resulting in the charges the ICC brought against Bashir. Estimates of casualties range up to several hundred thousand dead and millions were forced to flee.

However, Sudan was not party to the Rome Statute establishing the ICC. The Arab League and the African Union condemned the warrant and, since the indictment, Bashir has visited several countries that are party to the Rome Statute without being arrested.

Bashir was re-elected in 2010, though the election was marred by boycotts and reports of widespread intimidation and fraud. Meanwhile Bashir reportedly embezzled $9 million which was siphoned off to Lloyd's Bank in London. In 2017, he traded gold mining concessions, and gas and oil exploration rights with Yevgeny Prigozhin for the support of his Wagner Group mercenaries.

After months of protests and civil unrest, Bashir was removed by a military coup in 2019. He was arrested for killing protesters. Convicted of corruption and money laundering after $130 million was found in his home, he was sentenced to two years in prison. Sudan's new ruling military council agreed to hand Bashir over to the ICC. But when further unrest erupted in 2023, he was moved from prison to a military hospital.

# Life and Crimes

**1944** Born 1 January in Shendi, Sudan.

**1960** Joins the army

**1975** Appointed military attaché to the UAE.

**1981** Returns to assume military command.

**1989** Seizes power.

**1998** Writes new constitution.

1999  Sends army to quell opposition in parliament.

2003  War in Darfur breaks out.

2005  Ends civil war by allowing autonomy of South Sudan.

2009  Indicted for war crimes and crimes against humanity by the ICC.

2010  Indicted for genocide by the ICC.

2011  South Sudan becomes independent.

2019  Ousted by military coup and arrested for corruption.

2023  Moved from prison to military hospital.

# Samuel Doe
◄ 1951–1990 ►
## DICTATOR OF LIBERIA

Born in Liberia in 1951, Samuel Doe enlisted in the army at the age of 18. Trained by US Special Forces, he rose to become a master sergeant by 1979.

Like many indigenous Liberians, he resented the privileges garnered by the descendants of the freed American slaves who had founded the colony in 1822. On 12 April 1980, Doe and 17 other soldiers staged a pre-dawn attack on the presidential mansion in the capital Monrovia, killing President William R. Tolbert and 30 other government officials.

Seizing control of the government, Doe promoted himself to general and commander-in-chief. Heading the People's Redemption Council, he suspended Liberia's 133-year-old constitution and had 13 of the former president's associates summarily executed. Members of his own Krahn tribe took over all important positions.

Following an attempted coup, Doe held elections in 1985. Despite accusations of vote-rigging and intimidation, a special election committee determined that he had won 51 per cent of the vote. On 12 November, Doe survived another coup attempt. In retaliation, the army went on the rampage. Reports of human rights violations soared and there were charges that millions of dollars of US aid had been 'mismanaged'.

By 1989, the country was in a state of civil war. In July 1990, rebel forces advanced into Monrovia and their leader Charles Taylor demanded Doe's resignation. He refused and peace negotiations were conducted by the US and the Liberian Council of Churches. Five African nations sent troops to keep the peace, but the attempt did not succeed. After being wounded in a gunfight, Doe was captured and died under torture soon after. Charles Taylor took power and presided over a period of strife until his resignation in 2003. The election of Ellen Johnson Sirleaf in 2005 marked a turning point in the history of this ravaged nation.

# Life and Crimes

**1951**   Born 5 May in Tuzon, Liberia.

**1969**   Joins the army.

**1980**   As master sergeant stages coup.

**1980–1985**   Brutally suppresses opposition and installs his own tribe in top jobs.

**1985**   Rigs election.

**1985–1989**   Allows army to loot the country.

**1989**   Civil war breaks out.

**1990**   Refuses to resign; captured and tortured to death 9/10 September.

# Charles Taylor
### ◄ Born 1948 ►
## DICTATOR OF LIBERIA

Sentenced to 50 years imprisonment in 2012, Charles Taylor was the first former head of state to be convicted by an international tribunal since Hitler's successor Karl Dönitz at the Nuremberg Trials in 1946. However, the crimes he was found guilty of were committed, not in Liberia but in neighbouring Sierra Leone.

Born in Arthington, Liberia, his mother was an indigenous African while his father was reportedly an Americo-Liberian descended from freed American slaves. He went to university in the United States, graduating from Bentley College in Massachusetts in 1977. He returned to Liberia and joined Samuel Doe's coup in 1980 and became director general of the General Service Agency which handled government purchasing. In this position he was able to embezzle $1 million.

Fired in 1983, he fled to the US where he was arrested. Fighting extradition, he escaped from jail. Taylor later said that he had been assisted by the CIA. It was later reported that the Defense Intelligence Agency (DIA) used him as a source.

He turned up in Libya where he became a protégé of Colonel Gaddafi and received military training. With Libyan money, he started an uprising to overthrow Doe across the border from Ivory Coast, sparking the First Liberian Civil War. The breakaway Independent National Patriotic Front of Liberia captured Doe and tortured him to death.

The civil war ended in 1996. The following year Taylor was elected president with the slogan: 'He killed my Ma, he killed my Pa, but I will vote for him.'

He purged Doe's Krahn people from the army. Taylor then accused Krahn ally Roosevelt Johnson of plotting a coup and massacred his supporters. Hundreds fled. In 1999, the Second Liberian Civil War began. Meanwhile another civil war was raging in neighbouring Sierra Leone with Taylor backing the Revolutionary United Front. He armed them in defiance of United Nations sanctions with weapons bought with blood diamonds. At the same time, Taylor embezzled nearly $100 million, roughly half of total government revenue.

In June 2003, the Special Court for Sierra Leone (SCSL) charged Taylor with war crimes and crimes against humanity. The following month Liberia's capital Monrovia was under siege by the rebels. Then when an African force led by Nigeria and backed by the US landed, Taylor resigned and went into exile in Nigeria.

The US Congress put a £2-million bounty on his head. He appeared on Interpol's Most Wanted list and Liberia's new president Ellen Johnson Sirleaf requested his extradition. Taylor disappeared but was caught trying to cross the border into Cameroon. Arrested he was handed to the SCSL where he faced 11 counts of war crimes and crimes against humanity. He was sent to The Netherlands for trial.

Taylor refused to appear in court where he was accused of ordering atrocities in both Sierra Leone and Liberia. A pregnant woman near to term was cut open. Another was buried alive. Troops were encouraged to practise cannibalism to create fear among his enemies. Severed heads were put on sticks at roadblocks and human intestines were used as rope. He was also accused of murder, rape, amputation, mutilation and the use of child soldiers.

In 2006, he was found guilty of all charges. He was then sent to the UK which had agreed to imprison him.

## Life and Crimes

1948    Born 28 January in Arthington, Liberia.
1977    Graduates from university in the US.
1980    Joins Samuel Doe's coup.
1983    Dismissed from government for embezzlement.
1984    Arrested in the US.
1985    Escapes from jail and flees to Libya.
1989    Begins First Liberian Civil War from Ivory Coast.
1990    Doe captured and killed.

**1991**  Sierra Leone Civil War begins with Taylor backing the RUF.

**1996**  First Liberian Civil War ends.

**1997**  Taylor elected president of Liberia.

**1999**  Second Liberian Civil War begins.

**2003**  Taylor charged with war crimes and crimes against humanity; flees to exile in Nigeria.

**2006**  Taylor sent to The Netherlands for trial.

**2012**  Taylor convicted on all counts and sentenced to 50 years.

## Picture credits